A MAGICAL DREAM OF SCARAB DIVINATION

. . . When I awoke from this dream [of sacred scarab divination in an ancient Egyptian temple], I thought it was a gift from the gods, especially Isis. My attentiveness to the magic of scarabs seemed to allow them to manifest everywhere, and since that night's dreaming, I've had many magical experiences with scarabs.

While this book was being written they were out in great force, and the local scarabs (a bright metallic-green variety) were abundant. A festival I was attending chose the scarab as its symbol; scarabs flew in to join rituals; everywhere I looked they were being employed as decorations, or in jewelry, or as forehead *bindis*. It was definitely time to share this bright energy with everyone. May the sacred scarabs bring you enlightenment, insight, and joy.

—*deTraci Regula*

GW00401672

ABOUT THE AUTHOR

A student of the sacred sciences since childhood, deTraci Regula explores the mystical through writing, dreams, and art. She has been a priestess of Isis with the international Fellowship of Isis since 1983. Author of *The Mysteries of Isis* (Llewellyn, 1995), deTraci also produces and directs videos, writes on various magical and spiritual subjects, and has traveled to sacred sites in Greece, Turkey, China, Japan, and Britain, as well as the United States. Visit her website at http://www.geocities.com/Athens/Academy/7133

ABOUT THE ARTIST

Kerigwen is a full-time illustrator and has been sculpting in acrylic clays for twenty-five years.

TO WRITE TO THE AUTHOR & ARTIST

If you wish to contact the author or would like more information about this book, please write to the author in care of Llewellyn Worldwide and we will forward your request. Both the author and publisher appreciate hearing from you and learning of your enjoyment of this book and how it has helped you. Llewellyn Worldwide cannot guarantee that every letter written to the author can be answered, but all will be forwarded. Please write to:

deTraci Regula and Kerigwen
℅ Llewellyn Worldwide
P.O. Box 64383, Dept. 0-7387-0108-4
St. Paul, MN 55164-0383, U.S.A.

Please enclose a self-addressed stamped envelope for reply,
or $1.00 to cover costs. If outside U.S.A., enclose
international postal reply coupon.

Many of Llewellyn's authors have websites with additional information and resources. For more information, please visit our website at http://www.llewellyn.com

SACRED SCARABS

FOR DIVINATION AND PERSONAL POWER

deTRACI REGULA

ART BY
KERIGWEN

2001
Llewellyn Publications
St. Paul, Minnesota 55164-0383, U.S.A.

First Edition
First Printing, 2001

Disclaimer: While readings performed with the sacred scarab oracle are entertaining and often enlightening, they are not meant to replace professional advice of any kind.

Book design and editing by Rebecca Zins
Cover design by Gavin Duffy
Scarab designs and interior scarab illustrations by Kerigwen

Library of Congress Cataloging-in-Publication Data
Regula, deTraci.
    Egyptian scarab oracle / deTraci Regula ; art by Kerigwen.—1st ed.
        p. cm.
    Includes bibliographical references and index.
    ISBN 0-7387-0108-4—ISBN 1-56718-561-4 (kit)
    1.   Fortune-telling by scarabs.   2.   Scarabs.   3.   Amulets.   4.   Egypt—Religion.
I. Kerigwen   II. Title.

BF1891.S38 R44 2001
133.3'248—dc21
                                                                                00-054969

Llewellyn Publications
A Division of Llewellyn Worldwide, Ltd.
P.O. Box 64383, Dept. 0-7387-0108-4
St. Paul, MN 55164-0383, U.S.A.
www.llewellyn.com

 Printed in the United States of America on recycled paper

Other Works by deTraci Regula

The Mysteries of Isis
Llewellyn, 1995

Herb Magic featuring Scott Cunningham (video)
(directed by deTraci Regula)
Llewellyn, 1987

Whispers of the Moon (with David Harrington)
Llewellyn, 1996

Contents

These hieroglyphs, as seen on the cover, form part of the *Hymn for Sunrise*; this particular excerpt means:

[Osiris . . . maketh adoration to his Lord] . . . the Lord of Eternity, and saith: Homage to thee, O Heru-khuti, who art the god Khepera, the self-created. When thou risest on the horizon and sheddest thy beams of light upon the Lands of the South and of the North, thou are beautiful, yea beautiful, and all the gods rejoice when they behold thee.

A Note from the Artist

I had read deTraci's article in the *Magical Almanac* on how she had been given the idea for the Egyptian Scarab Oracle through a dream. Her description of the system and Tom Grewe's clear illustrations suggested a solution to my Yuletide gift-giving dilemma . . . I would make scarab sets for everyone!

Having created press molds and stamps for a couple of different glyph systems prior to this, I already had the tools and materials to begin the work. All I needed to do was copy the illustrations onto small ingots of acrylic clay so that the images would be reversed. I traced the illustrations for that first set with a fine marker onto tracing paper, then reduced the images on a copier (no computer then). Once the images were reduced to the right size, I retraced them using a medium lead heavily applied to a new sheet of tracing paper. Acrylic clay will grab a dry transferred image a lot like Silly Putty, making it easy to rub the traced illustrations onto the clay's surface in mirror images to the originals.

There followed a great deal of rolling and sculpting some rather fine lines and the making of a scarab mold to hold the clay while it is being stamped . . . to make a long story short, the sets were finished sometime way after Yule, and some of the recipients were friends I had made at Llewellyn while freelancing as an illustrator. These same friends were kind enough to put me in contact with deTraci, who was seeking to further develop her vision of a living divination system. After several reworkings (both of the text and of the prototypes), the project was deemed ready for production!

Now, through the grace of the Goddess and the diligent work and faith of many kind souls, these scarabs have now been guided into your hands . . .

Imbolc, 2001
Kerigwen

INTRODUCTION

THE ORIGIN OF THE EGYPTIAN SCARAB ORACLE

The Egyptian Scarab Oracle emerged in a very Egyptian way—through a magical dream. One night, after studying ancient Egyptian writings while I was writing *The Mysteries of Isis* (Llewellyn, 1995), I dreamed I was a young priestess at a huge temple complex dedicated to Isis. It was the night of a festival, so many people from the nearby town and the merchants traveling on the Nile were visiting the temple. Torches and lamps illuminated the high pylon gates and cast flickering shadows on the sandy ground surrounding the temple. Inside, hundreds of people were milling around, enjoying the music and dances and other entertainment. My eye was caught by a handsome young foreigner, a trader from far away. He was returning my attention, but I was very shy and I also didn't want to incur the wrath of the priestess in charge of training the young women. She was a striking but stern older woman, disdaining the wigs of the other women and priestesses, choosing to keep her own gray hair and outlining her eyes strongly with kohl. Rumor had it that she had a warm heart, but all the young priestesses were terrified of her. Still, I couldn't help flirting just a little and feeling the strange flush of energy, not unlike what I experienced in temple rites, flood through me when he would return my shy looks with bolder ones of his own.

Then, to my luck, the high priestess herself announced that there would be a sacred game: a divination by scarab. Everyone hushed as she explained the diversion. Scarabs would be scattered into the room, and we each were to grab whichever scarab touched us and then take it to her to be interpreted. So saying, she showed us a chest containing several hundred carved scarabs of every color, material, and description. Some had the heads of animals or humans, a few were carved out of stone, many were faience clay in different colors. She placed these scarabs into the center of a sparkling, finely woven net. Picking it up carefully so the scarabs wouldn't spill, she gathered the corners of the net into one hand, and then began to swing it rapidly above her head.

Suddenly, she let loose of one corner and the scarabs took flight, pelting us all. With laughter, everyone grabbed for a scarab. One hit the trader I admired and, bouncing off of him, landed on me, scooting down into the folds of my dress and catching at the base of my spine. I wiggled, trying to free the scarab, and he tried to retrieve it without creating embarrassment for both of us, but the resulting tangle caught the attention of the high priestess. She came over to us, demanded to know what we were doing, and we sheepishly explained. Only one scarab had touched the two of us; it was meant for us both. With a frown, because she neither liked foreigners nor her priestess-students marrying too young, she told us that the scarab indicated a wedding. We were delighted with this interpretation and decided to make it a truthful prophecy (probably to the relief of the high priestess, as I sensed that in this life I was not the most serious of her students, being more devoted to romantic dreams than to temple studies).

When I awoke from this dream, I thought it was a gift from the gods, especially Isis, granddaughter of Khepera by one sacred genealogy. My attentiveness to the magic of scarabs seemed to allow them to manifest everywhere, and since that night's dreaming I've had many magical experiences with scarabs. While this book was being written they were out in great force, and the local, living species, a bright metallic-green variety, were abundant. A festival I attended chose the scarab as its symbol; scarabs flew in to join rituals; everywhere I looked they were being employed as decorations, or in jewelry, or as forehead *bindis*. It was definitely time to share this bright energy with everyone. May the sacred scarabs bring you enlightenment, insight, and joy.

NOTE TO USERS OF THIS BOOK

The Egyptian Scarab Oracle has appeared in several forms. It first was included in Llewellyn's 1996 *Magical Almanac* as a twenty-scarab set. New research into temple divination systems of Egypt led me to expand the set for *The Mysteries of Isis*, where it appeared as a twenty-nine scarab set. After much meditation and years of using the oracle myself, and comments from other users, I made a few changes, most notably removing the Crescent of Isis scarab, as I felt it to be mainly redundant with the Throne of Isis scarab. It was replaced by the Feather of Maat as I felt an internal, divine pressure to include this symbol. I also added the Serqet scarab for this edition, primarily because Serqet/Serket was very insistent. If there is a deity or symbol that you feel should be included, feel free to add another scarab to represent it. The original dream that inspired this set involved hundreds of individually different scarabs, far more than could be included in any commercially produced set.

Any system of divination is a language of communication between us and the divine. Whatever words you add to this symbolic lexicon will help make it uniquely yours, and more powerful for your personal use.

May the sacred scarabs provide you with insight!

THE ART OF DIVINATION AND MAGIC IN ANCIENT EGYPT

The civilization of ancient Egypt, the world of the "Two Lands" united by the shining strand of the Nile, was a place that exuded magic and mystery at every turn. Every breeze, every flight of birds, even the random arrangement of lotuses in a temple pond or the movements of a sacred bull as he wandered in his paddock, all of these reflected the divine presence that pervaded the land.

With wisdom, these revelations of the divine will could be interpreted so that one could live peacefully—in accord with Maat, the divine rightness—so that the heart was clear and light, and life itself was balanced and filled with beauty and sacred awareness. To live in Egypt was to live in the temple of the world, a divine land whose inspired temple servants had mastered all the many arts of magic, divine communication, and divination. By words of power, or *hekau*, like gods themselves they could command the elements, contact the gods, and bring forth new creations.

For the average person living in Egypt, the temples themselves were forbidden places, whose high pylon gates would rarely open and whose innermost sanctuary was only open to the high priest or priestess and one or two other exalted god-servants. Once a year, on a festival for a high holy day, the divine statue would be brought out of its sanctuary and exposed to both the life-giving rays of the sun and the adoration of the folk who worked the fields, fashioned the goods, and served the god-king, the pharaoh. On these occasions, the movements of the holy image might be interpreted as the answer to a heart-spoken question, or a query could be posed directly to the priests carrying the divine statue.

Would the statue shift slightly for yes, or tilt another way for no? Temples with renowned oracles drew huge crowds for these festivals. The Nile would be busy with brightly decorated boats sailing up to dock at the temple quay, where everything, even the mooring post adorned with the head of a goddess, was imbued with the magical power of the temple beyond.

But the human need for sacred guidance couldn't be compressed into one or two moments a year, and then, as now, divination belonged both to the highly trained clergy and to the inspired folk magician. Outside, in the cooling shadow of the temple walls, arts of divination might be offered anytime in exchange for a piece of cloth, a sack of onions, or a little jar of oil.

Closer to home, Grandmother might know a bit of magic, using a lump of wax, a piece of thread, a few grains of sand scraped from a temple stone, or even a symbol to draw in ink on a scrap of linen to make a request or attract the benevolent attention of a deity. Some of these pieces of folk magic have survived for millennia. Even today, Egyptian women press together balls of dough on the eve of *Lelat al Nuktah*, Night of the Drop, the ancient Egyptian *Gerekh en Haty*, the holy night when the tears of Isis began to cause the Nile to swell against its banks. Making one for each member of the family, the women set them by the threshold to dry overnight. In the morning, the pattern of the cracks is carefully inspected. A ball too smooth means few years remain for its owner; one filled with many strong cracks presages a long life, long enough to earn many more wrinkles through the passage of years.

Many methods of divination involved children, believed to be naturally pure and closer to the divine world they had inhabited before their recent births. Their information, whether psychic or mundane, was considered reliable—even Isis, looking for the body of Osiris, sought the advice of children to guide her on her journey. Elaborate rites required a young person to scry in a pool of ink in a darkened room, and give the report of what they saw in the shining surface.

A less ritually inclined person with an important question could wander by the outer walls of the temple at lunchtime, when young scribes would be playing near the gates. Passing the happy, shouting children, a question would be repeated in the mind. The next random words heard as the children played their games would serve as the divinely inspired answer. In the beliefs of Kemet, the "Black Land" made livable by the dependable return of the fertilizing Nile, everything vibrated with living magic, and so anything might show the divine will. A question or request would be formed, and then anything that caught the attention could indicate the divine answer, or at least divine attention—a bird crying out, the waving of temple banners in the breeze, and even the flights of scarab beetles sparkling in the sun were subject to excited scrutiny.

Khepera, the Divine Scarab of the Sun

With a large scarab beetle serving in place of a head, the human form of the sun and creator-god Khepera is strange to behold. Even in his beetle form, the wings are sometimes falcon wings rather than those of the beetle itself. Beetle or bird, Khepera's multicolored wings were believed to provide the brilliant colors of both the dawn and sunset skies, and he grasped the round globe of the sun and pushed it into the sky, where he rolled it all day and then guarded it all night. Khepera was the Sun God, supreme long before Ra, Amun, or Aten, a self-creating and constantly transforming deity whose very name came to mean "becoming, transforming, and creating." But how did a beetle, and a dark one at that, become a symbol of the all-creating Sun God?

The answer lies in the mysterious habits of the *Scarabeus sacer*, one of several species of beetles in Egypt that caught the attention of the inhabitants. These beetles gather their favorite food, the dung from oxen and cattle, and roll it into huge spheres, which they push around and fight to keep safe from the predations of jealous beetles. Female beetles laid their eggs in a similar ball, providing food for the young beetles when they emerge. All positive attributes were assigned to the beetles—they were creative, protective, and they seemed to prefer to roll their movable feasts from east to west, like the movement of the sun. The small beetle easily rolling its huge dung ball may have even inspired the invention of the wheel, a great gift to lighten the labors of humankind. Early observers believed that all beetles were males. In this view, like gods, they sprang self-generated from the rich mud of the Nile. In the heat of the day, when all other creatures took to the shadows, brightly colored, metallic-bodied beetles took to the sky in flight. In evening, like the sun setting, they would find a safe, hidden place for the night.

With all this magical potency, the scarab became the supreme symbol of life to the Egyptians, far surpassing even the ankh as a magical amulet and symbol of life. In the preparations for the afterlife, Yves Cambefort believes that the process of mummification and the diagonal wrapping of many mummy bandages may have been done in imitation of the larval form of the beetle, decorating the human body in hopes that the spirit would enjoy the same seemingly magical transformation the beetle achieved, changing from worm to pupa and then to winged being with full powers of flight. The wrapped body swathed in linen strips does resemble the pupal stage of the beetle, when the hard outside shell conceals the fluid rebirth taking place inside as the wormlike grub gains its wings. Carol Andrews cites a view held by some Egyptologists that even the structure of Egyptian tombs was based on the vertical shaft and horizontal chamber the female beetle constructs to safely hold her pear-shaped egg ball.

Physical and spiritual transformation and the freedom to assume any desired form was a crucial part of the many rites contained in the Book of Coming Forth by Day. The deceased initiate could follow the divine instructions to become a swallow, a falcon, a lotus, or the winged beetle itself. As divination tools, the scarabs once again bring that same power of personal transformation.

THE SCARABS IN EGYPT

For the Egyptians, carved or molded images of scarab beetles served several purposes and can be divided into four different types. These are scarabs for identification, scarabs that honor or commemorate an important event or person, funerary scarabs, and scarabs used in jewelry and as amulets. The identification scarabs bear a name, sometimes with an inscription or symbol. As the Egyptians often sealed objects and doors with knotted ropes over which a clay lump was pressed, the scarab was an easy-to-carry sealing object that could be pressed into the wet clay. If anyone broke through the seal, the assault was unmistakable. The sealing scarabs, since they were distinctive, assured that the door or object could not be simply resealed after the theft. Letters were sealed by rolling up the papyrus, tying it with cord, and then pressing a sealing-stone into the wax or clay seal.

Many scarabs bear the name of pharaohs, sometimes those of dynasties many centuries older than the tombs in which they were found. The Egyptians, like us, were fascinated by ancient times and would sometimes try to re-create the art and images of past golden ages. It is believed that scarabs bearing the names of long-past pharaohs were part of this desire to honor and restore the "good old days." Sometimes a single scarab would contain the name of the current pharaoh paired with one from a past dynasty, rather like modern American politicians posing with an image of Lincoln or Washington in the background.

In some cases, the presence of a king's name on a scarab is the only individual record we have of his existence, which has enabled archaeologists to correct and expand lists of kings. Always holy, deceased pharaohs were considered to be especially divine, so carrying the name of a pharaoh on a scarab may also have functioned as an amulet designed to attract the attention of the new god.

Although only a few types exist, the so-called historical scarabs were issued to commemorate and publicize important events. In essence a durable form of press release, these big scarabs were carved with tales of the prowess or accomplishments of the Pharaoh Amen-hotep III, made in many copies, and distributed throughout the country and to vassal states beyond the borders. This custom died out after his first son, first known as Amenhotep IV and then as the "heretic pharaoh," Akhenaten, issued his own commemorative scarabs. Future pharaohs shunned the practice.

Scarabs were carried as good luck pieces and exchanged as gifts, usually with formulaic good wishes, like "Happy New Year"—making them a durable form of an early greeting card. Others bore the name of a god or goddess, such as "Amon Is My Strength," intended to bring the energy and particularly the protective powers of the deity to the person who carried it.

While scarab seals were worn as rings, they were also incorporated into other jewelry. Necklaces were formed of different-colored scarabs strung together, protecting the neck of the wearer and, perhaps, ensuring the continual renewal of beauty.

Most of the early funerary scarabs produced were tiny, often only about half an inch long. One exception was the heart scarab, a much larger scarab that was placed on the throat or chest of the mummy. Sometimes called "The Heart of Isis," use of the heart scarabs arose during the tumult of the Hyksos Period, apparently under King Sobekemsaf of the Seventeenth Dynasty. When so much of Egyptian culture was at risk, thoughts of rebirth in a better place were even more important to the Egyptians, and so yet another protective amulet was created.

The heart scarabs are usually inscribed with a magical spell known as Spell 30B, expressing the wish of the heart's owner that no obstruction to salvation would emanate from the heart itself.

Even during Ankhenaten's reign, when many funerary customs were forbidden as heresy, scarabs were still placed with mummies. They were often inscribed with the "nefer" sign for happiness, accompanied by a fish symbol.

One papyrus document shows the proper distribution of the various funerary amulets that were placed on the body or within the mummy's bandages. In addition to the heart scarab and pectoral scarab, eight or nine other scarabs were laid within the wrappings, providing their powers of protection and regeneration for the parts of the body beneath them.

Different areas produced very distinct scarabs, even though the kilns were only a few miles from each other. Tanis provided schist scarabs of poor quality and decayed glazes but nearby Nebesheh created clay scarabs sparkling with a light-green glaze. Scroll-bordered scarabs were the special creation of Abydos, ancient center of Osirian worship. Fashionable styles changed from dynasty to dynasty, resulting in a wonderful variety over time. Some experts on insects can discern the different types of beetles used as scarab models.

Scarabs were exported to other countries, and local imitations soon sprang up as the bugs became popular additions to funerary customs. They are found at many sites in the Holy Land that were under Egyptian control, and further east into western Asia. Their small size made them perfect souvenirs, and they were carried to many places, often ending up incorporated into local burials. Scarabs found their way into tombs and gravesites throughout the Graeco-Roman world and beyond, into the "barbarian" lands. Even then, the allure of ancient Egypt and the fame of its sacred magic made many who may not have ever heard the names of the Egyptian gods still want to possess their token in the underworld . . . just in case things worked out differently than they expected.

As with many things Egyptian, earlier examples are mysteriously of higher quality than many of the later versions. Pioneering researcher Flinders Petrie notes that Khufu's Fourth Dynasty (c. 2630–2510) scarabs are small and beautifully made, with fine, durable coloring, but only two kings later, by the time of Khafra, the finer points of the art of glazing were lost. This loss of quality continued until the Eleventh Dynasty, when permanent, hard glazes of good color enjoyed a revival. By the next dynasty, these advances were already slipping away again, and the colors were not as permanent. The common brown scarabs excavated in great numbers began their magical lives as bright green beetles, and a similar transformation occurred with most white scarabs, which started out as blue.

Petrie was one of the first to seriously study scarabs, though he was afflicted with a curious blind spot regarding forgeries. Despite working in a time when local entrepreneurs had seen the foreign passion for scarabs, and were reproducing them on a vast scale with increasing cleverness, Petrie insists that, "Generally speaking, forgeries—except of one or two obvious kinds—are very rare, and there is nothing like the amount of doubt in the matter which is supposed to exist."

T. G. Wakeling devoted twenty-eight pages to tales of forged scarabs, including those that had fooled experts. He writes, in *Forged Egyptian Antiquities* (Adam & Charles Black, London, 1912), that "it is now extremely difficult for even well-known Egyptologists to give a definite statement concerning the genuineness or otherwise of a specimen submitted to them." He adds that forgery is nothing new—we have no way of knowing if the "re-issued" scarabs made a thousand years after the reign of the king they commemorated were passed off to unsuspecting Egyptians as the real thing. Think about this if you are tempted to spend several hundred dollars to buy a "genuine" ancient scarab for your collection!

Forgers with consciences sometimes would go to the extent of making new scarabs out of the ground-up paste of unattractive ancient ones, or glazing them with chipped-off glazes from damaged or less desirable antiquities. Or small gemstone scarabs were created out of beads found in tombs. Facing a gullible buyer, the seller could happily swear that the scarab is genuinely old.

In some cases, the newly made scarabs make a visit that would please real-life beetles, who rely on the nourishment provided by the dung of animals. To age these modern re-creations, the completed scarabs are buried in a dung heap, then oiled, covered with dirt, and finally carried around by the forger to give them convincing signs of wear.

Modern Egyptian scarab manufacturers are said to feed their scarabs to penned turkeys, who later deposit them, suitably aged, for the benefit of their keepers. Since the scarab beetle deposits its own eggs in a ball of dung, this method of creating new scarabs also has an odd resonance with the original beetle! Before this method grew in popularity, a good aged patina was obtained by burying them in wet sand, earth, and ashes.

Most of the scarabs made today are too obviously of modern manufacture to be confused with the real thing. Present-day scarab dealers find a ready market for reproductions. Most gemstone scarabs used in jewelry are cut far away from Egypt, in Hong Kong or other parts of Asia. Hieroglyphic inscriptions are reduced to a few suggestive scribbles, scarcely recognizable and almost invariably unreadable or without meaning.

THE MAGICAL BEETLE OUTSIDE EGYPT

The special attention granted the beetle was not limited to Egypt. Over a quarter of a million types of beetles are known, ranging from the infinitesimal to huge specimens the size of toy cars, sporting horns like rhinoceros. Many of them are important in creation stories, perhaps because of the worldwide myth of the creation of humans by a deity forming us out of damp clay. The many dung beetles who live their lives seeking moist excrement may have been thought appropriate companions for the creation deities, and sometimes took their places in the myths. One of these is Aksak, a South American beetle deity who formed the Chaco tribespeople out of clay. Tales from Southeast Asia and India tell of a scarab who dives through the swirling waters of primeval time, grasps some earth from under the waters, and uses it to form dry land, creating the stage for the emergence of land animals and humans.

The English word "beetle" comes from the Old English *bitela*, meaning "biting." While most beetles don't prey on humans, some of them can deliver a nasty bite. They are often classified in literature with the so-called noxious creatures, such as the spider and scorpion. Shakespeare includes them when the fairies sing asleep their queen in Act II, Scene II of *A Midsummer Night's Dream*:

You spotted snakes with double tongue,
Thorny hedgehogs, be not seen;
Newts and blind-worms, do no wrong,
Come not near our fairy queen.
Philomel, with melody
Sing in our sweet lullaby;
Lulla, lulla, lullaby, lulla, lulla, lullaby:
Never harm,
Nor spell nor charm,
Come our lovely lady nigh;
So, good night, with lullaby.
Weaving spiders, come not here;
Hence, you long-legg'd spinners, hence!
Beetles black, approach not near;
Worm nor snail, do no offence.

Elsewhere, the bard presents a more sympathetic beetle:

Darest thou die?
The sense of death is most in apprehension;
And the poor beetle, that we tread upon,
In corporal sufferance finds a pang as great
As when a giant dies.
(from Act III, Scene I of *Measure for Measure*)

In modern times, scarabs are often incorporated into necklaces and rings, and imitation heart scarabs are carved from soapstone and used as paperweights. Something of the old magic still clings to scarabs. New Age folklore credits the faience scarab with the ability to absorb stray radiation from computer monitors. The quartz in the clay is supposed to draw the emanations into the body of the scarab, thus protecting the computer user. Nearly two thousand years ago, Roman writer Pliny wrote that the green color of scarabs was believed to be restful to the eyes, and noted that the gemstone carvers kept them nearby to prevent eyestrain. Modern scientists have found that the human eye is best adapted to see green, so gazing at a green scarab may in fact be good for the eyes. Whether or not they are effective against radiation is another question.

Before low-radiation monitor screens became commonplace, a bright turquoise faience scarab stood guard for me. Whether it was psychology or magic, its presence seems to make a difference, and though I don't consciously use it as a radiation amulet anymore, it still decorates my desk. As an ancient symbol of the sun, which constantly consumes energy, perhaps the scarab is an appropriate choice to also consume harmful rays. And perhaps the Egyptians used scarabs as amulets because they, too, found they made a difference.

DIVINATION WITH THE EGYPTIAN SCARAB ORACLE

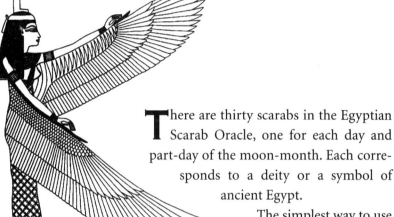

There are thirty scarabs in the Egyptian Scarab Oracle, one for each day and part-day of the moon-month. Each corresponds to a deity or a symbol of ancient Egypt.

The simplest way to use the scarab oracle is to form a question in your mind, and then draw a scarab from the pouch. This method has ancient precedent; divination by rings, some of them holding scarabs, was used in Roman times. The rings of military officers were gathered together and placed in a bag or other vessel. A question pertaining to the military situation at hand would be asked, and then one ring would be drawn forth. The image on the ring was then interpreted to provide the answer to the question. The oval shape of most incised gemstone seals is derived from the shape of the inscribed base of the popular scarab.

You can also spread the scarabs out facedown in front of you. With this method, simply pick up the first scarab that attracts you, identify the image on it, pay attention to your own intuition pertaining to the symbol, and then, if you wish, look it up in the meanings given here. If, when you touch the scarab, you get an impression or answer that is different from the ones given here, pay attention. We all have our own divinatory languages, and meanings and interpretations can vary widely and wildly. What the scarab reveals to *you* is the answer that has the most relevance for your question.

Since the vast majority of readings fall into six categories, specific meanings for each scarab are given for love, health, career, money, family, and spiritual path readings. Scarab associations with places, times, and people are also provided to give more detail to your divinations.

After the reading, if you want to emphasize and integrate the answer you received, carry the sacred scarab with you for a day. If you would like to explore the answer in the dreamworld, try placing the scarab under your pillow for three nights, taking care to record your dreams, no matter how bizarre, in the morning. This method can give you remarkable insights, and is especially useful in major life-change divinations, when we look for insight into what we need to do with our lives at a given time.

Basic information on the Egyptian meaning of each symbol is given in the section "The Egyptian Scarab Oracle," page 29. This is only a starting place; the more you enhance the meanings and information given here with your own studies, meditation, and experience, the more accurate and revealing your readings will be.

If one of the deity symbols keeps appearing in your personal readings, it may mean that you have a spiritual resonance with the deity represented. Exploring this relationship may be very fruitful for your spiritual development. Also, the more you learn about these deities, the more accurate your readings will be as you become accustomed to their symbols, powers, and stories.

In addition to the general types represented by some of the deity scarabs, individuals of any gender or age may be represented if they share a prominent trait with the god or goddess. For example, a life-long-career military man might still be represented by Horus or Sobek, even if he is elderly and long away from the battlefield. Or an astrologer might be represented by Nut, or a healer or doctor by Isis.

Never read for the same question again on the same day, unless events have already transpired that change the initial situation. Even if the answer seems wildly impossible, meditate on it before asking the same question again. Oracles must be treated with respect; if you constantly reject what is revealed to you, eventually you will receive no information at all. You can, however, ask about a related question, or for more clarification. Just don't keep drawing scarabs until you get the reading you wanted, disregarding all that has gone before. You may eventually get to experience that outcome, but you could find yourself working through every other reading you rejected first.

When giving a reading, remember always that the person sitting before you is often in a delicate state of mind, impressionable and ready to believe. Even if he or she is not approaching the reading seriously, doing it only as entertainment or on a whim, what you say can have a great impact. If a reading appears to indicate a negative outcome that distresses the querent, work with them and suggest how negative influences can be modified . . . *and they always can be.* Even the ancient Egyptians believed in the power to constantly modify and purify their souls of evil intention, influences, or their own past misdeeds. One could always work to "lighten the heart," and so get by the scales of judgment. With positive readings, point out how the good outcomes can be strengthened and made more likely.

During the time spent doing the reading, you are acting in the place of a priestess or a priest of ancient Egypt, with similar responsibilities. Choose your words carefully, honestly, and tactfully.

While readings performed with the Egyptian Scarab Oracle are entertaining and often enlightening, they are not meant to replace professional advice of any kind.

A DIVINATION RITUAL

As with all divination systems, the more prepared you are to ask the question, the more enlightening the answer will be. While the Egyptian Scarab Oracle is perfect for quick readings, ritual environments enhance the experience. Clear and create a sacred area using whatever methods are comfortable for you. Ideally, there should be a vessel of fresh water nearby as an offering to the water that makes all life possible, and a lit candle. Breathe deeply for a few moments before beginning.

Then offer sweet incense to the scarab god Khepera or to Isis (or another, preferably Egyptian, deity with whom you have empathy). Pick up the pouch holding the scarabs and pass it reverently through the smoke of the incense. If you can't use incense, let a few drops of an essential oil or inspiring perfume fall onto a stone or crystal, and pass the scarab pouch over the sacred scent. Ask for guidance in using this oracle. Say the words of the invocation below or use similar ones of your own choosing, either aloud or in your mind.

Invocation to Isis and Khepera

> *Great Goddess of Light,*
> *Lady of green things,*
> *Bringer of the sacred breezes,*
> *Bring to me the insights needed*
> *As I consult your sacred oracle.*
> *Let me enjoy clarity of vision,*
> *Compassion of heart,*
> *And wisdom of the soul*
> *As I seek the answer to this question: (ask question).*
>
> *Bright Lord Khepera,*
> *Dark sun, glowing sun,*
> *Shine on me and let me explore*
> *What I seek to know, and more.*

Let me enjoy brightness of spirit,
Speed of action,
And knowledge of eternity
As I seek the answer to this question: (ask question).

If reading for another, substitute "bring to us," "as we consult," and so on for the singular version given above.

State the question and wait a moment. Listen to your mind—are you already modifying the question, or trying to guess the result? Sometimes at the moment of divination we finally realize exactly what outcome we most desire, and that can also be a powerful insight. Are you asking the right question at the right time? Are you clear and calm enough to read for someone else, if that is the case? State the question again, and wait a moment longer. Finally, state the question once more. If at any point you substantially modify the question, state the new, modified question three times in succession.

Now scatter the scarabs in front of you and choose one, or simply draw one from the pouch. For more detailed readings, draw three scarabs—for the past, present, and future, and for insight into what you've been, what you are now, and what you are becoming. Or use one of the multiple-scarab layouts described on page 19.

Perform your reading and note down the scarabs and the insights you receive in a small notebook. Meditate quietly on the answer you have received. Then gather up the scarabs, thank the spiritual forces you have invited for attending, and end the rite by blowing out the candle.

Interpretation is an art; while many meanings are given for the scarabs in different contexts, the supplied meanings are only the beginning. Your unique associations and experiences with the symbols will guide you to your own understanding. A scarab that seems negative to one person may be very positive to another, or may relate in a completely different way depending on the person receiving the reading. Trust your own intuitions, even if they do not concur with the provided possible meanings.

SAMPLE READINGS WITH
SINGLE SCARABS

Question: Will I get the office job I applied for?

Answer: Seshat.

Possible Interpretation: Yes, since Seshat controls writing and accounting. But be aware that accuracy will be very important, and check to make sure all of your applications and other paperwork are correct.

Question: Will my relationship with X work out?

Answer: The Incense Bowl.

Possible Interpretation: Possibly—it's in your hands (just like an incense bowl being offered) and depends on the amount of energy you are willing to put into the relationship, or "offer," like incense for the gods, to the place of romance in your life.

Question: Will my investments do well this year?

Answer: Nephthys.

Possible Interpretation: Unlikely. Double-check your financial situation—a partner may not have been honest with you. (Nephthys loved Osiris, but was married to Set, and was unfaithful to him. But Nephthys can also be viewed in a more positive light.)

Question: Where should I go on my vacation?

Answer: Anubis.

Possible Interpretation: The desert (haunt of jackals in Egypt).

Follow-up Question: What desert?

Answer: The Temple.

Possible Interpretation: Go to a sacred area of desert, such as the Grand Canyon (which has a rock formation called "The Temple of Isis"), or to a spiritually active place like Santa Fe or Sedona. If finances permit, go to Egypt itself.

SAMPLE READINGS WITH MULTIPLE SCARABS

Pyramid Reading

Formulate your question and draw out three scarabs. These represent the "base" of the situation, the influences affecting the outcome. Draw two more scarabs. These represent the "construction" of the pyramid—what you can do working with, or against, the base influences. Draw a final scarab. This represents the outcome of your efforts, the "apex" or best that can be attained in this situation.

Row 3:		6		
Row 2:	4		5	
Row 1:	1	2	3	

This reading is particularly useful when you are dealing with a number of outside influences in a given situation.

Example: What career should I pursue?
Here are the scarabs that were drawn:

Row 3:		Ankh	
Row 2:	Bast		Temple
Row 1:	Ibis (Tahuti)	Sistrum	Nile

Row 1 shows that you have mathematical and/or accounting skills (Tahuti), along with a flair for music and dancing (the Sistrum). But the Nile shows that you like to let things flow along easily, something not particularly compatible with mathematics and accounting.

Row 2 reinforces the gift for music and dancing (Bast), and gives discipline in the form of the Temple. You appear more willing to give your best energy to your creative arts, rather than to your mathematical gifts.

Row 3 gives the Ankh, symbol of life and a positive outcome. As music and dance might be considered more lively than math, you should follow your natural inclination to pursue a career in the arts, particularly dance, since the Ankh is a symbol of the motion of life as well. With the Temple and the Sistrum (sacred instrument played in the temples) present in this reading, your dance activities will be a form of service to the divine. Since you do have the gift for mathematics, accounting, and writing, you will find that your efforts will be successful financially as well. Also see the Double Arc of Nut reading (page 22) for a deeper exploration of talents and challenges.

Temple Reading

This reading is good for any questions regarding two individuals or two opposing points of view. Draw eight scarabs, laying them out alternately in two vertical lines, beginning at the bottom and working up. Draw three more scarabs, 9, 10, and 11, and set them between the two lines, forming a crossbar at the top. This represents the pylon gate of the temple. Then add the two doorway scarabs, 12 and 13.

Row Four	7	9	11	10	8
Row Three	5				6
Row Two	3				4
Row One	1				2
Row Five		12	13		

Scarabs 1 and 2 represent the base of the opinions or viewpoints. These are the essential backgrounds, and cannot be easily changed or modified. Scarabs 3 and 4 show how the two individuals regard themselves. Scarabs 5 and 6 show how the two individuals regard each other. Scarabs 7 and 8 represent the attitudes now coming into play. Scarabs 9 and 10 represent what each individual or side is likely to do in relation to the other. Scarab 11 represents the outcome of these actions. Scarabs 12 and 13, forming the gateway, indicate whether the two sides will ultimately be in harmony or in opposition.

Example: I'm having trouble with my boss at work. Will I be fired? Here are the scarabs that were drawn:

Row 4	*Anpu*	*Horus*	*Pyramids*	*Barque of Ra*	*Nut*
Row 3	*Nile*			*Nephthys*	
Row 2	*Osiris*			*Bast*	
Row 1	*Cobra*			*Shen*	
Row 5		*Set*	*Khepera*		

Row 1 shows that the two sides are definitely in opposition. One, Wadjet the Cobra, favors quick, decisive action, and is willing to do almost anything to achieve results. It is also a symbol of royalty—if this person is not in authority, then arrogance may be a problem. The other, represented by the Shen, symbol of eternal cycles, prefers to let things work out over the long term.

Row 2. The Cobra-based column believes itself to be the victim (Osiris, who was torn to pieces by Set). So the Cobra column probably represents the person having the reading. The Shen-based column believes itself to be pleasant and fair, forgetting that it can sometimes be vengeful or capricious (cat goddess Bast, more interested in having a good time than doing work, and not above toying with a mouse for the pleasure of it). This looks to be the "boss" column.

Row 3. The Cobra column has a lot of energy, and is reliable (the Nile, ever-flowing giver of life to Egypt). Properly controlled, it can be very productive.

The Shen column goes behind people's backs and can be deceptive (Nephthys betraying her husband, disguising herself as Isis to sleep with Osiris).

Row 4. The Cobra column is going "underground" (Anpu, the guide of the underworld) and is being very meticulous (Anpu, carefully wrapping mummies), but is not satisfied. The Cobra side will be gradually getting angry, self-righteous, and warlike (Horus).

The Shen side, Starry Sky of Nut, is distancing itself from the situation, just as Nut could only be reached by letter during the disputes between Set and Horus. It's waiting for the right moment to take action, and when it does, it will be with full authority (the Barque of the Sun god Ra) though, like Ra, the opinions of others will be taken into consideration, albeit begrudgingly.

The Pyramids are a sign of stability and also represents organizations. While the boss, represented by the right column, may have been offended, and may even write you up (sending letters to Nut, as the gods did in the myth of Horus and Set), the basic situation will remain stable. They don't want to lose you, and you don't want to lose your job.

Row 5. The Gateway. Ultimately, the two sides will remain in opposition. You still feel offended, angry, and victimized (Set, who in his own mind was the victim of Osiris) and they are just flying along, content in their authority (Khepera, the flying beetle who is another manifestation of Ra). While the situation is stable for the time being, you will want to look for work in a more congenial environment, or try to change your attitude to the job.

Double Arc of Nut Reading

Based on the travel of the sun through the day and nighttime bodies of Nut, this is a very potent reading that is a good introduction to working with the Egyptian Scarab Oracle and can provide detailed insights.

If you wish, select a scarab as a significator to represent yourself or the individual for whom you are reading. When reading for yourself or an individual who is present, this scarab can be omitted, but it is helpful for distant readings. You can look through the scarab "people" descriptions to make your choice, or simply choose on that feels right to you. Or go by these suggestions:

Boy or Young Man	Horus
Girl or Young Woman	Bast
Adult Man	Min, Osiris
Adult Woman	Isis, Seshat, Nephthys, Serket

Older Woman, Female Authority Figures   Nut

Older Man, Male Authority Figures   Barque of Ra

Place it on the table in front of you. Say these or similar words:

> *For the length of this reading you represent (name of quer-*
> *ent). You stand in for (name of querent) and the insights I*
> *obtain will pertain to (name of querent). We are all mixtures*
> *of light and dark, shadow and sun, body and spirit, con-*
> *sciousness and unconsciousness.*

Lay out ten scarabs in an oval around the significator, if you are using one, starting on the left and continuing clockwise. Begin the reading with the first scarab. It represents a person, influence, or situation that is just beginning to "ascend" or make itself felt. This is the dawn or rising sun. The second scarab represents existing conditions or people which are becoming more important. The third scarab represents the noonday sun—the most powerful, dominant influence at this time. The fourth scarab indicates a recently potent influence which is now beginning to decline. The fifth scarab is what is passing, the setting sun. It may be leaving the picture entirely, or sinking into the subsconscious where it will continue to exert a subtle influence. It could be a job that is ending, a relationship whichi is passing or changing, or a hobby, couse of study, or spiritual path which is no longer right for the person to follow. This is the dusk, or setting sun.

The sixth scarab may be either a new force just distantly beginning to affect the person's life, or an old one which has little effect on conscious life at this time, though it may still be part of the unconscious motivations affecting the person. The seventh scarab is an influence which may be positive or negative, but is still being formed on the subtle levels of the soul. It could be a dream, a desire, or a character challenge or a new strength. The eighth scarab is the "Midnight Sun," a potent influence in the subconscious. It affects the "Noonday" scarab, either strengthening it when it represents a similar force, or balancing it when it represents an opposite. If positive, it strengthens and enhances the individual in many ways. If negative, it may be a challenge point that affects almost every aspect of life.

The ninth scarab is an influence or belief that has been subconscious, but which is now beginning to shift toward the conscious and mundane worlds. The tenth scarab may be a spent force that is leaving the person's cycle entirely and will no longer have a subconscious influence, or it is waiting to break into the upper consciousness as a "dawning" scarab.

Write down the scarabs drawn, if you wish, and do your interpretation. At the end, gather up the scarabs of the arcs first. Then pick up the significator and say these words:

> *During this reading you have stood for (name of person).*
> *Now you return to your own beingness, without taint of other*
> *consciousness. You are the scarab (name of scarab). I thank*
> *the energies of the universe in guiding me in my reading.*

As with all readings, the scarabs and the conditions they represent will change over time. Even the action of having a reading can start changes in consciousness that change our attitudes and, with them, future possibilities.

For a more detailed reading, increase the number of scarabs in the arcs up to twenty-four, one for each of the twelve hours of the day and of the night.

There are two positions where "new" influences may enter, at the first descending position below the horizon, and at the first ascending position above the horizon. This is where the energies are least stable and these scarabs can shift—a descending scarab may not go below the horizon, but may halt the flow of the scarabs behind it. A rising scarab may not quite make it to the horizon—another influence may push it away or block it. The entire "sky" of scarabs may be moving very slowly, or very quickly; this can only be determined by subsequent readings over time.

Scarabs may also "exit" without entering the supreme position, or may go through that spot so quickly that their influence is diminished or not perceived at all. For additional insights, read the opposing scarabs as pairs. The Ankh and the Sistrum, both of which can symbolize benevolent, lively activity, form one such pair. In this particular reading, Isis and Osiris would form one pair, emphasizing a present or past relationship. Anubis and the Union of Isis and Osiris form another pair, one which does not seem particularly positive. It is not necessary to read these scarab pairs, but doing so can deepen the interpretation and is helpful when things seem obscure on the surface.

Example: This is a general life path reading for a man who has recently made substantial life changes in almost every area. He is a writer by trade.

Here are the scarabs that were drawn:

3: Seshat

2: Anubis   *4: Horus*

1: Crook and Flail of Osiris   *5: Sistrum of Hathor*

above the horizon

---

below the horizon

10: Ankh   *6: Isis*

9: Starry Sky of Nut   *7: Union of Isis and Osiris*

8: Tahuti

The first scarab, dawning above the horizon, is the Crook and Flail of Osiris. This indicates a quieter time of reflection. In some ways, the person may feel that they are the victim, but at this time, there is not much that they can do. This process can also be an initiatory one.

The second scarab, ascending, is Anubis. This emphasizes the quiet period, where many things have gone "underground" or into the "underworld." Conscious life may be continuing apparently smoothly but underneath things are being felt deeply and examined carefully. It is a time of initiation and meditation. Both these two scarabs are somewhat passive and intense activity is not recommended now. Great changes are probably past, at least for a while.

The third scarab, highest in the "sky" as the dominant "noonday sun" influence, is Seshat, lady of writing. It is likely that a literary or research project is foremost right now.

The fourth scarab, descending, is Horus. This may be a son of the person, or it may represent an attitude, a Horus-type person, or the divine influence of the hawk god. This influence will soon be waning, but for the present, it is still strong. Anger or irritation may be frequent, and there is a low tolerance for frustration.

The fifth scarab, Hathor's Sistrum, is one whose influence is weakening and about to go under the horizon or out of the cycle entirely. This may refer to a relationship, particularly a sexual one. This will not be as important in the near future. Work, rather than pleasure, will probably be dominant.

Under the horizon, in the sixth position, is the Isis scarab. Recently strong or just entering the cycle, it will be sometime before this exerts a strong influence. Exactly opposite to the Osiris scarab, it may eventually be an influence which helps "put it all together" as Isis reassembled Osiris.

Deeper under the horizon in the seventh position is the Union of Isis and Osiris. An important relationship is now less so in the everyday world, but it still exerts its influence in the subconscious, an influence which will either increase as it moves into the "Midnight Sun" position, or it will fade away.

Echoing Seshat above, Tahuti is in the dominant eighth position below. Writing work is likely to be very important for some time to come—if Seshat sets, Tahuti may be rising, and this literary, intellectual attitude is shared by both. Writing is probably the most important thing to the person right now, both consciously and subconsciously. Both these scarabs could also apply for accountants and mathematicians, as they are both involved in calculations as well, but as this individual is a writer, it seems much more likely that they are here referring to a writing project.

The Starry Sky of Nut is beginning to make its influence felt as it ascends toward the horizon line in the ninth position. This will bring many things, mostly positive. Astrological influences will be strong. As the Starry Sky is between two very positive scarabs—the Ankh and Tahuit—this influence should be a very beneficent one.

The Ankh, symbol of life and the full power of life, is just below the horizon in the tenth and final position. After an almost deathlike period, where Osiris and Anubis hold sway, a "new" life is waiting to ascend with all of its power.

Summation: At present, this man is in a time of reflection that will result in new and deeper insights. The writing work is very strongly supported and is the most important thing to him at this time and for a long period to come. A relationship appears to be passing or becoming less important, though this may change eventually. Astrological influences will gradually become more favorable, and his "new life," while not yet quite begun, will be a pleasing and happy one.

THE EGYPTIAN
SCARAB ORACLE

1. The Lotus

In cultures worldwide, the lovely lotus is a symbol of enlightenment and joyful understanding, representing spiritual unfolding, rebirth, love, beauty, and the peaceful resolution of difficulties. The lotus has its roots in mud, stretches up through murky, stagnant water, and then bursts into glorious bloom in the sunshine or, in some varieties of water lily, by night and moonlight. The fragrance is mildly intoxicating, believed to be an aphrodisiac. The sacred pools that accompanied virtually all of the larger temples in Egypt contained lotuses and water lilies, and were used by the priestesses and priests for purification. Blue lotuses were worn by the Egyptians as headdresses and carried for their scent. Nefertum, son of Ptah and Sekhmet, was the Egyptian god of perfumes and was said to have been born in a lotus blossom. Like Khepera, Nefertum could represent the emergence of the sun in the morning sky.

After death, Egyptians hoped to be able to take on the form of the lotus, and the eighty-first chapter of the Book of Coming Forth by Day was devoted to the spell that could transform the deceased into the flower. "I am the pure lotus which springs up from the divine splendor that belongs to the nostrils of Ra," one version states. Another praises the flower itself: "Hail, Lotus! . . . I am he who knows you, and I know your names among the gods, the lords of the Duat, and I am one of you."

This scarab always indicates a good time to meditate and study sacred subjects.

Possible Meanings in Different Types of Readings

Love: Rough or dark beginnings followed by positive outcomes and long-term happiness. Often indicates relationships that initially face opposition from friends and families. The Lotus scarab suggests that individuals can overcome their problems and ultimately succeed in drawing strength from their dark side while blossoming in the light.

Money: Improvement in finances, good returns on investments, wise expenditures. A good time to make important purchases, such as cars and houses.

Career: This scarab indicates abundance unfolding after a dark or murky beginning. Problems at work can be outgrown—don't rush to change jobs, but possibly change your attitude.

Family: The lotus indicates a period of general happiness. An infant may be born or adopted, or an older child may be joining the family.

Health: Good health, or a positive outcome to treatment, particularly when new health awareness is created.

Spiritual Path: New insights or pathways are opening to you, and you are receiving the benefit of past spiritual efforts from this life or others.

Types This Scarab Can Represent: People who have survived hardship and succeeded, individualists, and exceptionally beautiful or enlightened people of either gender.

Timing: January, or the first month of any calendrical system. The first day of the month, the first day of the lunar cycle, or the first day of the week.

Location: Rivers, riversides, marshes, moist regions.

2. Sobek the Crocodile

Sobek is an unpredictable but often benevolent deity worshiped in the marshy, croc-infested regions where he is sometimes said to be the husband of Isis or Hathor, or the son or husband of Neith, potent warrior goddess of Sais.

In the afterlife, a pharaoh sought to become like Sobek and enjoy his privileges. Utterance 317 of the Pyramid Texts is titled "The King Becomes the Crocodile-God Sobek":

> *I have come today from out of the waters of the flood; I am Sobek, green of plume, watchful of face, raised of brow, the raging one who came forth from the shank and tail of the Great One who is in the sunshine.*

Sobek served as a symbol of the royal power of the pharaoh, who could strike suddenly, effectively, and without mercy when necessary. Occasionally, he is considered a form of Set, who did take the form of a crocodile on occasion. The Sethian association with Sobek is not defined in the original myths and derives from Sobek's powerful, aggressive qualities.

This scarab represents dangerous or difficult to control forces, unexpected mishaps or accidents, and unseen forces beyond casual control. It can predict the entry of new individuals into one's life, with challenging or difficult results. When this scarab comes up, be alert and meditate often to prevent or limit difficulties.

Possible Meanings in Different Types of Readings

Love: Can indicate love with an individual you have never before noticed suddenly emerging into your consciousness, like a crocodile rising from the water. Beware of placing too much importance on first impressions, either positive or negative.

Money: Dangers for the unwary. Watch your wallet, physically and financially. It may indicate lotteries and gambling, but not always with good results.

Career: Watch out for backbiting at work. Positions require the ability to take decisive action. May indicate jobs with the military, as soldiers or others acting in the service of military authority. Career choices may involve swimming, diving, hunting, submarines, the maritime industry, and marshland or ocean preservation.

Family: The Sobek scarab can hint at unsuspected problems and substance abuse. With children, it can show the potentially negative effects of competition. Expect sudden changes.

Health: Strong or sudden intervention may be necessary to preserve or restore health. Operations and hospitalizations. Emergency treatments, broken bones, injuries.

Spiritual Path: The crocodile, although frightening, is well adapted to its surrounding environment and capable of fierce defense as well as predatory attack. Realistic, philosophical spiritual explorations will be more appealing at this time than purely mystical ones. Energetic, physical methods of approaching the spiritual are indicated. Some martial arts systems combine all of these and can be very appropriate for Sobek-scarab individuals. In spiritual matters, the presence of this scarab may also mean that the person receiving the oracle must be more assertive in order to make progress spiritually. It can also refer to problems in the spiritual "family," the group or school surrounding the individual.

Types This Scarab Can Represent: Individuals, especially males, who may not reveal their true natures, or who act suddenly and out of character. Decisive individuals who go their own way.

Timing: February, or the second month of any calendrical system. Second day of the month, second day of the lunar cycle, or second day of the week.

Location: Rivers, oceans, lakes, marinas, watersides of all kinds.

3. THE PALM TREE

The sacred palm oases of Osiris offered sanctuary, rest, and cool water to inhabitants and travelers in the desert. He was called Lord of the Palm Grove and the palms, with their abundant, sweet dates, were sacred to him. As with other trees, anyone who cut down one was believed to be angering Osiris. The crossing of palm fronds sometimes forms a perfect five-pointed star, and may have been the original inspiration for the symbol of the pentagram, which originated in palm-rich territories such as Egypt and Sumer. It is believed to be protection from bad weather wherever it is grown, which is probably true in the desert regions it favors.

In general, this scarab can denote travel and vacation. It is a scarab of fruitfulness and plenty. However, it can also denote isolation, as the distant oases were sometimes used as places of exile from the richer world of the cities along the Nile. It can represent faraway places, distant relatives, and foreign lands.

Possible Meanings in Different Types of Readings

Love: Standing alone, the Palm Tree brings a period of solitude. In an existing relationship, it can show the need to retreat from the world with your loved one.

Money: The oases of Egypt are fertile places in the middle of the desert. Despite appearances to the contrary, resources are or will soon become available.

Career: This is a time when you may need to voice unpopular opinions at work. Assignments may require working in isolation, or at locations far away, even overseas. Business travel and jobs in the tourism industry are other possibilities.

Family: The Palm Tree shows a vacation or other peaceful period, away from problems. It can mean visits to relatives, generally well-liked and pleasant ones. However, it can also mean standing alone and feeling isolated from the family.

Health: In health matters, the Palm Tree can indicate convalescence or the need for retreat to reduce stress and maintain health. It's a good time to visit a health spa, preferably one far from cities. The palm is a sign of fertility and bodes well for the conception of children.

Spiritual Path: The quivering fronds of the Palm Tree speak of introspection and relaxation. You will generally prefer going your own way and standing up for your beliefs. Retreats, especially to isolated locations, will recharge your spiritual batteries.

Types This Scarab Can Represent: Isolated individuals, retired people, those involved in travel, religious recluses, distant relatives, friends living far away or in foreign lands.

Timing: March, or the third month of any calendrical system. The third day of the month, the third day of the lunar cycle, or the third day of the week.

Location: Oases, secluded areas, desert watering holes, islands with palm trees, and resorts fitting these descriptions.

4. The Throne of Isis

Isis is a supreme, universal, mother goddess, multifaceted, called the Goddess of Ten Thousand Names in an effort to include her many aspects. Also a goddess of wisdom, war, and space, she is most often invoked as a goddess of love, family, magic, and healing. In Egypt, she was the protectress of the throne, which is the symbol she wears on her head. The throne headdress of Isis is a powerful and positive scarab.

Isis' skill as a magician was employed when she sought to receive the sacred true name of Ra, her father in some stories. Ra was ignoring the needs of humanity and Isis resorted to a drastic act of magic, creating a small snake from the exudation of his body, which bit him. To stop the pain, Ra agreed to give Isis his most secret name, allowing her to restore balance.

Her faithfulness and love shine through in the story of Isis and Osiris, where the pair rule Egypt until Osiris' brother Set arranges to murder him and take Isis, the transmitter of the power of the throne, for himself. Isis, heartbroken, finds Osiris and brings his body back to Egypt, where Set discovers his corpse and savagely hacks it to pieces. Isis, with Anubis, binds Osiris' body together and restores him temporarily to life, enabling her to conceive their son Horus. Horus, too, is attacked by Set, but Isis saves his life. After many battles, Horus conquers Set and is recognized as the legitimate heir of Osiris, worthy to receive the power of the throne.

If cast in answer to a question, this generally denotes a positive, joy-ful outcome for the person asking the question.

Possible Meanings in Different Types of Readings

Love: Generally denotes the blessing of the goddess. If unattached, look for her assistance in matters of love, as she can be an effective matchmaker.

Money: Positive outcomes but all goals must be tenaciously pursued.

Career: Usually, this scarab shows that you are enjoying the benefits of good management and prosperity. It indicates a good time to ask for a raise or promotion, if you are qualified. Isis, as queen, was a top manager in all senses, and her scarab can be very favorable for those who are seeking such positions, or who need the assistance of the boss in an endeavor.

Family: The Throne of Isis scarab represents protection and defense of the family. While very positive for children and for healing, it can suggest disputes over inheritances and other conflicts between the adults in the family unit.

Health: The presence of the symbol of the divine physician Isis indicates that health will remain strong or, if presently ill, healing will occur.

Spiritual Path: In spiritual readings, the Throne of Isis scarab can mean that goddess energy in general, or the Isis energy in particular, will be a very positive path for the individual receiving the reading. As with all the scarabs carrying a deity symbol, the presence of the scarab of Isis may indicate that the reader is fulfilling a modern portion of the Isis mythos. Keywords to consider in this connection are quest, travel, just battle, determination, love, and faithfulness. As someone who has loved and lost, the presence of this scarab indicates comfort if you are alone, and the healing of grief. For followers of Isis, it may also indicate a need to get out of the way of the goddess and let her create the resolution she desires for you. Isis represents women in all phases of life and beyond. For men, she represents the ideal, divine woman. She also represents healers, doctors, and health-care professionals of either gender.

Types This Scarab Can Represent: Strong women, wives, mothers, women politicians, leaders, enchantresses, and healers.

Timing: April, or the fourth month of any calendrical system. The fourth day of the month, the fourth day of the lunar cycle, or the fourth day of the week.

Location: Egypt, Cairo, Alexandria, and capital cities all over the world.

5. Crook and Flail of Osiris

The Crook and Flail of Osiris were part of the ritual equipment of the pharaoh and of Osiris. The crook denotes guardianship and protection; the flail is an instrument of harvest used to beat the grain from the straw. Osiris both protects and pushes. For ordinary people, the Crook and Flail served as a funerary amulet that was said to endow them with the same powers of dominion as the pharaoh and, by extension, of Osiris.

Osiris is the Lord of the Underworld, slain by his brother Set and restored, temporarily, to life by his sister-wife Isis, who searched for his body and reassembled it after Set had torn it to pieces. The presence of the Osiris scarab speaks of initiation and of nonphysical concerns. The presence of a deity scarab may also indicate that the reader is fulfilling or interacting with one of the portions of the Osiris myth cycle. Keywords to consider here are stagnation, isolation, opposition, and initiation.

The interpretation of the Osiris scarab also depends on the relationship of the reader to the different aspects of Osiris. Since most of the surviving inscriptions concentrate on the important funerary and initiatory aspects of Osiris, the common perception of him is a tomb-bound, gloomy one. But just as Isis can be perceived as perpetually in search of Osiris' body or perpetually mourning him, Osiris can also be perceived as continuously alive in an eternal moment where Set's attack has yet to occur. Seeing him this way, Osiris is a lively lover exhilarated by music and dance and the intoxication of his love with Isis. The Greeks associated Osiris with Dionysus, leading dances and enjoying music. Seen in his entirety, Osiris represents all men in all phases of life and beyond, and can symbolize both men and women who have passed from this life.

Possible Meanings in Different Types of Readings

Love: Generally positive for love and committed relationships. However, it may indicate a time of separation. Career issues may take precedence over romance or family, which may damage or change relationships.

Money: Pay close attention to how your money is being managed. Double-check investments, accounts, tax returns, and bills you are paying. Experts may not be telling you the whole picture. Long-term investments are favored.

Career: The actions of others may be thwarting your efforts. Don't believe everything you hear. You may be left out of the loop; chase down information you need and verify it.

Family: Since Osiris was forcibly separated from Isis, this scarab can mean that separations are possible, though generally not willing ones. Young children need careful nurturing and protection. Squabbling relatives.

Health: Rest and convalescence will be required; recovery may be slow.

Spiritual Path: Initiation. Soul retrieval. Casting off the material in favor of the spiritual. A time of turning inward. Study of the afterlife, reincarnation, and the Book of Coming Forth by Day, the Tibetan Book of the Dead, and similar works are useful.

Types This Scarab Can Represent: Men in general, husbands, mates, male politicians. Convalescent individuals, individuals at the end of life, or those already in the spirit world.

Timing: May, or the fifth month of any calendrical system. The fifth day of the month, the fifth day of the lunar cycle, or the fifth day of the week.

Location: Underground areas, caves, hospitals, ancient sites with tombs.

6. SESHAT, LADY OF WRITING

Seshat is the sacred goddess of writing and of measuring, the divine recordkeeper of the royal house and the pharaoh. She is the one that lays out the cords to guide the builders of temples and, some say, she is the one who holds the measuring string of life as well. Her symbol is an enigma, variously interpreted as a seven-pointed star or a seven-petaled flower, both contained in an upside-down pair of horns hovering above the goddess' head, resembling a bell jar placed over the "flower."

The presence of this goddess' scarab can indicate that it is time to take action before opportunity is lost. There is also an implied caution to be certain that the work is begun on a solid, well-measured foundation.

The Seshat scarab represents writers, builders, and creators of all kinds.

Possible Meanings in Different Types of Readings

Love: Express your emotions through letters and writing. Take note of special days and anniversaries—don't miss them. Ask and answer questions to make sure there are no misunderstandings.

Money: Check your recordkeeping and be sure it is accurate and complete, especially in records kept by others.

Career: Any career emphasizing communication will be successful. Very favorable for jobs involving writing, recordkeeping, mathematics, lettering, calligraphy, libraries, and bookstores. Also favors architecture, construction, city planning, and government work.

Family: Communicate in writing to build closeness and to avoid misunderstandings. Keep up on paperwork, school records, and medical records, and check these for errors.

Health: Search for more information and confirm results of exams or tests. Go for top-quality care by experts. Keep a diary of how you feel.

Spiritual Path: Explore knowledge through old and new books and by meditating on sacred writings. Experiment with dowsing, research ley lines, and employ feng shui. Create poems and new sacred writings.

Types This Scarab Can Represent: Writers, mathematicians, teachers, and librarians of either gender.

Timing: June, or the sixth month of any calendrical system. The sixth day of the month, the sixth day of the lunar cycle, or the sixth day of the week.

Location: Libraries, offices, universities and colleges, places with official or national records, such as the Library of Congress in Washington, D.C.

7. The Shen

The shen is the sign of eternity, of endless cycles, and of the travel of the sun across the sky, endlessly repeated. The original shen was a loop of papyrus rope bound to itself. A visual representation of a binding knot, it was also believed to protect whatever was placed within it. The cartouche surrounding royal names is actually an elongated shen, wrapping the name with protection, both from the knot and from the divine energies of the sacred papyrus that formed the original rope. Shens and blank cartouches were used as funerary amulets for ordinary people, conferring protection. These amulets were usually made of a dark stone such as basalt or, sometimes, deep blue lapis lazuli shot with pyrite, evoking the nighttime sky.

In art, the shen is often shown clutched in the talons of Nekhebet, the nurturing vulture goddess who is also the symbol and divine protectress of Upper Egypt, and who is sometimes associated with Isis. The shen can also be seen as a glyph of Geb, the earth god, stretched out horizontally below Nut, goddess of stars, arched over him. The Egyptians used the sign of the shen as the symbol for "ten million," a number vast as eternity, numberless as the stars.

The presence of this scarab in any reading usually means a delayed outcome.

Possible Meanings in Different Types of Readings

Love: Any romantic situation, good or bad, will continue unless a conscious decision is made to change it, and then implemented.

Career: The Shen represents day-to-day work, ongoing employment, and tedious but not particularly demanding jobs. If unsatisfactory, nothing will change unless a determined effort is made to do so. If satisfactory, no change is necessary to keep the job going.

Money: The Shen favors long-term investments, interest-bearing accounts, life insurance policies, and any cyclic, ongoing generation of income.

Family: Under the influence of the Shen scarab, normal routines will continue. Again, if the current situation is unsatisfactory, change will only come with focused effort.

Health: The Shen indicates no drastic changes for good or bad. But it can also refer to persistent conditions that resist treatment and to continuing health challenges. It can also suggest the practice of good habits intended to increase longevity.

Spiritual Path: The Shen suggests any sort of method relying on practice and repetition that will bring rewards and insight over the long term. Employ mantras, chanting, daily practices of yoga and tai chi, daily meditations, and similar practices.

Types This Scarab Can Represent: Rarely represents human individuals.

Timing: July, or the seventh month of any calendrical system. The seventh day of the month, the seventh day of the lunar cycle, or the seventh day of the week.

Location: Highways, railways, isolated long roads, enclosed communities, walled cities.

8. Tahuti the Ibis

Tahuti or Thoth is the god of wisdom and discernment. He is represented by either the baboon or the ibis, a small, black-and-white, marsh-dwelling bird. The black and white of its feathers were believed to refer to the phases of the moon, as did its long, crescent-shaped beak. It was Tahuti who came to the aid of the sky goddess Nut when Ra forbade her to give birth on any day in the year. He played a gambling game with Khonsu, the moon god, and won enough light to make five additional days so that Nut could bear her children.

Later, it was Thoth who came to the aid of Isis, helping her to flee from the mill where Set had imprisoned her. He assisted her in giving birth among the reeds, and also stopped the boat of Ra when her son Horus was bitten by a scorpion. Thoth conveyed to Isis magic words to restore the boy to life, and held back the boat—and time itself—until Horus was alive again.

Tahuti was also in charge of the calendar, marking off days on a palm frond sheared of its leaves. The House of Life, the scientific and magical repository of knowledge at the temples, was under Tahuti's special protection. He was later associated with Hermes under the name Trismegistos, the "thrice-great," a term that may have derived from one of Thoth's titles at Esna.

In a reading, this scarab indicates that the reader is to seek more information, to strive to act wisely and justly, and to seek imaginative answers to problems.

Again, as a deity scarab, the presence of Thoth may indicate that the reader is working through the Tahuti mythos as a counselor, a gambler, or as a divinely inspired energy.

Possible Meanings in Different Types of Readings

Love: Tahuti can act altruistically to assist others, gambling to gain enough light for Nut to give birth (see also the Starry Sky of Nut scarab entry) or assisting Isis in her escape from Set. In romance, look to friends who can help bring together individuals or offer counsel on existing relationships. If there are relationship problems, seek the help of others to act as mediators. This scarab can also indicate platonic friendships, where sex and romance are not involved.

Money: Tahuti was a gambler at times. A risky investment may pay off.

Career: The Tahuti scarab is very positive for any question relating to education, or to career changes requiring courses or additional study. Seek mentors and advice from others. Alliances will work to everyone's advantage.

Family: Relatives are a resource. Educational endeavors are rewarded. Children rise to challenges and exceed expectations.

Health: The Tahuti scarab prescribes that the patient, if ill, seek expert advice. Pay attention to advice of doctors, trainers, nutritionists, and other health instructors to maintain or restore optimum health.

Spiritual Path: Tahuti was the supreme scribe and master of the written word. Explore books for spiritual insight and training. Mathematical spiritual systems are ideal, such as Kabbala or sacred geometry. Work with the lunar energies as well as the solar ones and be attentive to cycles and astrological events.

Types This Scarab Can Represent: Teachers, advisors, counselors, gamblers, and outlaws. This scarab can also represent instructors, officers, and guides.

Timing: August, or the eighth month of any calendrical system. The eighth day of the month.

Location: Beaches, watersides, lakes.

9. Bast the Cat

Cat goddess of joy, Bast was sometimes thought of as the embodiment of the "soul of Isis," since the words Ba-Ast translate to that phrase. Bast was revered as a loving mother goddess and a less bloody form of the lioness goddess Sekhmet, a powerful defendress and goddess of war and destruction. However, at times, Bast herself could take on the form of a lion and there are many lion-headed amulets and statues that are inscribed with the name of Bast. Her primary symbol was the cat, which was used to indicate liberal sexuality and sensuality. She is often shown with her kittens at her feet or in a basket over her arm.

Bast's primary city was called Bubastis, named for her. Each year, an annual festival similar to Mardi Gras took place, with drunkenness, unclothed boat rides, licentious behavior, and other festival pastimes overtaking the city for the duration of the festival.

The essential and sometimes changeable independence of the cat makes this scarab subject to many interpretations, depending on the reader's own personality. Bast is usually positive in romantic readings, particularly those where sexuality, rather than romantic love, is most desired.

Possible Meanings in Different Types of Readings

Love: The presence of the Bast scarab is excellent for short-term or relatively uncommitted relationships and problematic for long-term and committed relationships due to lack of permanent commitment from one or both partners.

Money: General energizing of finances.

Career: Positive for artistic careers, dance, the theater, and graphic arts. Environmental preservation, wildlife preservation. Not good for boring jobs or work environments with close supervision.

Family: The Bast scarab usually indicates a loving environment for children. Short tempers and "cattiness" can disrupt tranquility, but blow over quickly.

Health: The Bast scarab suggests that stretching, dancing, yoga, and movement therapies will be potentially helpful. Exercise, but not to the point of exhaustion (and, of course, get plenty of rest and catnaps). But be careful—alcoholism and other problems resulting from overindulgence are sometimes indicated.

Spiritual Path: The presence of this scarab favors meditative pursuits but also upbeat, practical philosophies. Not a time to abandon material things in favor of spiritual pursuits. Explore ecstatic dancing, drumming, body work, and sacred sexuality.

Types This Scarab Can Represent: Independent women, often young. Can represent feline companions and wildlife in general. Women in general, particularly those who are free-spirited and/or changeable.

Timing: September, or the ninth month of any calendrical system. The ninth of the month or the ninth day of the lunar cycle.

Location: Natural surroundings, comfortable places, cozy retreats.

10. The Ankh

The ankh is the foremost Egyptian symbol of life and spiritual power. Egyptian gods and goddesses carry ankhs as evidence of their power to transmit and create life. Temple gate keys were sometimes made in the shape of ankhs. Deities and pharaohs are depicted being purified under a stream of ankhs flowing out of sacred vessels.

Various explanations of the ankh's form have been presented, varying from its likeness to a sandal strap (and therefore symbolic of the motion of life) to the outline of the female genitals, or the union of the male and female organs. One of the more logical explanations is that it derived from a stylized African fetish-doll called *aku*, which was carried to promote fertility. These round-headed dolls with short arms and straight sticks for bodies strongly resemble the ankh form, though no one knows which came first.

However, the origin of the ankh symbol was probably different from any of these and may remain unknown. In addition to being a symbol of life, the ankh is also a transmitter of force and spiritual energy, which is life in another form. Its presence in a reading is positive in virtually all circumstances.

While the ankh is a very popular modern symbol of ancient Egypt, it was not a mass-produced amulet. Compared to scarabs or other symbols, relatively few ankhs were made as amulets. Its primary use was in hieroglyphic inscriptions and occasionally as a decorative element.

Possible Meanings in Different Types of Readings

Love: Sacred unions, possibly resulting in pregnancy.

Money: The Ankh indicates abundance in financial areas, with sufficient resources for whatever is needed.

Career: Positions in healing arts, medical research, and environmental protection are emphasized. Increased activity at work, new clients, technologies, increases in staff, promotions and new assignments.

Family: New energy. Pregnancy and childbirth. Harmony and hope.

Health: Problems will be resolved and healing will take place.

Spiritual Path: Confirmation that you are on the correct path. Renewed devotion to spiritual practices, particularly those of ancient Egypt. Spiritual attainments, new skills and methods. Stimulation and balancing of the chakras, and mastery of healing energy systems such as polarity therapy and reiki. Ultimate enlightenment.

Types This Scarab Can Represent: Generally will not represent a human individual, though it can signify the state of being pregnant or indicate a recent birth.

Timing: October, or the tenth month of any calendrical system. The tenth day of the month or of the lunar cycle. Also the final day of the Egyptian ten-day week, which was celebrated as a holy day and day of rest.

Location: Sacred places, sacred buildings, gardens, parks, and waterfalls.

11. THE TEMPLE

The high pylon gates leading to many of the temples of Egypt announced the beginning of sacred space, of enclosure. The temples were the religious and administrative centers of Egypt, crammed with workshops, schools, offices, and slaughterhouses in addition to the sacred buildings. Most of these other buildings have not survived; only the sacred structure itself was made of durable stone. The temples were physical outposts of the pharaoh and his relations, the divine gods and goddesses.

The presence of the Temple in a reading may indicate that the reader is in or about to begin a period of "temple service," where esoteric duties must be discharged. Most sacred service in Egypt was performed by groups of priests and priestesses who worked at the temple one out of every three to four months, returning to their ordinary, secular lives in between these times of working devotion.

The temple scarab can also refer to other "sacred enclosures" such as the home or workplace. Explore any sacred aspects of the matter at hand to be sure you have examined the spiritual aspects as well as the material side of things. It can also be a reminder to take a necessary retreat from mundane concerns, and to work on refining your soul rather than merely earning your paycheck. The Temple can also represent established organizations of all kinds, such as companies, churches, banks, schools and universities, and fraternal organizations.

Possible Meanings in Different Types of Readings

Love: Relationships that have a sacred dimension, which may or may not be sexual/romantic. Divine union and sometimes marriage.

Money: Sufficient but not lavish resources, having enough for daily life without stress.

Career: Work for large organizations or corporations. Charity organizations, religious groups. Can indicate a calling as a religious services leader.

Family: Strengthening of relationships. Family gatherings. Religious and spiritual activities as a family. Ceremonies.

Health: Hospitalization or careful medical care may be required. Reduce stress.

Spiritual Path: The Temple scarab represents an active time religiously and spiritually. It is a good time for daily study and practices, and exploring traditional or ancient faiths. This scarab favors the establishment of ceremonies, rituals, and spiritual organizations.

Types This Scarab Can Represent: Reverends, priest/esses, and clergy of all kinds, especially those who speak for an organization, all of any gender. Other organizational authorities, the head office, company spokespersons, etc.

Timing: November, or the eleventh month of any calendrical system. The eleventh day of the month or of the lunar cycle.

Location: Sacred spaces and places, religious buildings, other organizational headquarters, universities, walled enclosures.

12. The Nile

The river Nile is the guiding thread of Egyptian culture, bringing life in all its forms to what would otherwise be barren. Its presence in a reading is generally positive. The Nile scarab suggests the Taoist approach to resolving difficulties by flowing around them like water. Look for less-active solutions to problems, including simply waiting for events to unfold. Eternal or cosmic flows, tides, and seasonal changes are also present in the Nile scarab.

The personification of the Nile was the god Hapi, who was represented in human form with a paunch and pendulous breasts, probably to indicate the fertility and fruitfulness that the Nile waters brought. Hapi was sometimes shown with the emblem of Upper or Lower Egypt on his head, or as a twin pair of deities, each wearing one of the symbols.

There were three seasons in Egypt, based on the flow of the Nile. The inundation was when the waters rose, flooding the land. Then came the time of planting, as the waters receded, leaving behind a new, rich layer of fertile silt. Finally, there was the harvest. All of these seasons varied along the length of the Nile, with the earliest flooding coming farthest south, nearest to the high mountains where the torrential rains of Africa nourished the Nile with water.

Possible Meanings in Different Types of Readings

Love: Hapi was sometimes shown with his twin, tying together the symbols of Upper and Lower Egypt. In love readings, the Nile scarab symbolizes lasting love flowing easily between the partners. It can also mean necessary travel in connection with a relationship, either for a visit or on a vacation.

Money: The Nile was almost perfectly reliable during the millennia of Egyptian civilization. For modern seekers, it indicates a favorable, consistent money flow.

Career: Like the river, try to go around problems rather than through them. The ancient Nile also suggests possible advancement by seniority and persistence, rather than by making big changes. Channel your energies effectively.

Family: The continuous flow of the Nile indicates normal growth and progress. As a bringer of water and so of food, it shows this is a good time for the nurturing of growing things—including children. In general, a peaceful, productive time for families.

Health: Gradual change. Problems related to water, elimination, digestion, and energy imbalances. Bathe or drink sacred or special waters to maintain or improve health.

Spiritual Path: This scarab recommends following a path of non-conflict and nonviolence. Taoist practices fit this description—go around the rock, instead of over or through it, as a river flows. Meditation and sacred travels.

Types This Scarab Can Represent: Generally, the Nile scarab does not represent a human individual.

Timing: December, or the twelfth month of any calendrical system. The twelfth day of the month or of the lunar cycle.

Location: All rivers of the world. Echoed in the sky by the Milky Way.

13. NEPHTHYS

Nephthys, shadowed by her sister Isis, oppressed by her brother-husband Set, and unable to entice her beloved Osiris save in her guise of Isis, can personify victimization and alert the reader of this potential or leaning. However, Nephthys grows to defy Set and allies herself with Isis, uniting with her in the resurrection of Osiris. In this sense, Nephthys frees herself, redeems her actions, and achieves a balanced goddesshood as a twilight deity, underworld goddess, and maker of dreams. She can represent young women, particularly those who are unmated or unhappy in relationships. In timing, Nephthys is the goddess of the dark of the moon and of eclipses. The scarab of Nephthys can indicate darker sexuality, desperate actions, and strife in marriage and other relationships. The presence of her scarab, as with the other deity scarabs, may indicate that the reader is fulfilling or interacting with her myth.

Nephthys can also indicate a person whose motivations are unclear or uncertain, or whose actions may, more or less innocently, bring harm. This scarab also indicates times and periods of transition, just as Nephthys is symbolized by the dusk, the time between night and day. In readings for both love and health, Nephthys indicates a difficult outcome. However, if Nephthys can be equated and balanced by her twin, Isis, her influence will be much more positive.

Nephthys has another side to those who know her well. She parallels the goddess Neith, her opposite in many ways. Neith could also be considered the consort of Set, but in her case, it was a much more even match. Warlike and aggressive, her name can be interpreted to mean either "that which is" or "the terrifying." Yet, at the temple of Neith in Sais—where Neith could also be combined with Nephthys' sister, Isis—the healing powers and physician skills of her priests were renowned. Some believe that Neith became Athena, the Greek goddess of wisdom, who nonetheless carries the shield of war.

Possible Meanings in Different Types of Readings

Love: Illicit love or sacred passion that breaks conventional bounds. Exploration of sacred sexuality.

Money: Hidden financial resources. Lavish and probably unnecessary expenditures. Listen to intuition. Be on guard against deception.

Career: Favorable for creative, independent careers. Unfavorable for traditional or narrowly defined jobs. Secondary roles, assisting others.

Family: Children with challenges, physical or emotional. Problems between adult brothers and sisters. The threat of infidelity, and mismatched or misplaced love. Divorces made necessary due to incompatibility, lack of love, and even violence.

Health: Challenges. Difficulties in childbirth and childbearing. Healing insights in dreams or by intuition. Illnesses caused by repression of natural desires and nature. Assistance from doctors.

Spiritual Path: The Nephthys scarab reminds us to listen to the dark as well as the bright, and of going within and exploring the subconscious. Spiritual practices that create changes in consciousness, psychic explorations, and astral projection work all come under the influence of Nephthys. Break away from conventional faiths. Inspired writings, channeling, and visions. Dreamwork.

Types This Scarab Can Represent: Women in unhappy marriages, battered wives, "other women," aunts.

Timing: Blue moons. The thirteenth day of the month or of the lunar cycle. Eclipses, lunar or solar.

Location: Houses and homes.

14. SET

Set was one of the five children born to Nut, goddess of the sky, and Geb, god of the earth. Set was impatient to be born and burst out of Nut's side early. This made him the first-born son, and those that have tried to justify Set in his battle against his brother Osiris point to his first-born status, however artificial it was. Violent and vigorous, Set is required to kill the Apep serpent that attacks the Boat of Ra each night. His power, though feared, was useful against other, more alien evils.

The presence of the Set scarab indicates great strife, unjust dealings, and prolonged litigation. Here is an oppressor in all senses, tolerable only as a controlled force to be used against greater or unknown evils. His nature is fiery, dry, and destructive. As a bringer of utter chaos he can in some cases liberate people or things caught in stultifying bonds, but he can also entrap individuals in those same bonds. His long-suffering wife, Nephthys, eventually goes over to the side of Isis and Osiris simply to escape from him.

For those sympathetic to Set, all these implications are different and Set is the oppressed, rightful heir to the throne of Egypt, cast aside in favor of a mere child suspiciously begotten on a dead king. In some early mythologies, his own legitimacy for the throne of Egypt was favored over that of Osiris. He represents adversaries in general or any aggressive, stubborn individual.

Possible Meanings in Different Types of Readings

Love: Unhappy or abusive relationships and harsh sexuality untamed by love. One-night stands and exploitative sexual relationships. Sudden, strong sexual urges. Chronic attraction to "bad boys" or "wild women"—or of *being* a "bad boy" or "wild woman."

Money: Losses due to theft or deception. Lost or disputed inheritances. Problems with relatives over money.

Career: Fights with bosses, or horrible bosses. Loss of jobs. Conflicts. Competitiveness, sometimes to personal advantage and gain but generally insufficient or wasted resources.

Family: Chaotic family life. Impatience with children. Harsh discipline and abuse. Rejection of children. Divorces, separations, infidelity.

Health: Indicates feverish conditions and injuries that will be difficult or time-consuming to heal. Sudden crisis in an existing condition, or the emergence of a new problem. Alcoholism, drug abuse, and similar conditions may cause problems.

Spiritual Path: Beware of being self-centered or of exerting domination of others in the name of religion. Breaking up of established groups or organizations. The outsider, the rebel. Perpetual discontent.

Types This Scarab Can Represent: Mean men, abusive husbands, unreliable associates, people who erroneously believe that they have been wronged and who may have chips on their shoulders as a result. In Egyptian tradition, red-headed people were associated with Set.

Timing: The fourteenth day of the month or of the lunar cycle.

Location: Deserts, desolate areas, oceans and other salt water.

15. THE STARRY SKY OF NUT

Nut is a primal goddess whose body is the arching, star-flecked sky, pulled apart from her mate Geb, the earth, in order to allow room for humanity on the surface. After Ra forbids her to give birth on any day of the year, she nonetheless gave birth to the five gods Isis, Osiris, Nephthys, Set, and Horus on days won for her by Tahuti, who gambled with the moon god Khonsu for a portion of his light. Her nature is cosmic and her presence in a reading indicates that there are great matters at hand, possibly beyond ordinary human control. In this sense, this scarab indicates a concept close to inexorable fate.

Though the Night of Nut is best known, she is also the arching day sky as well. At night, Ra sails through her body; during the day, he sails upon the blue waters of her daytime body.

The Nut scarab is a positive influence on any creative endeavor or new beginning, and is also positive for love and health. It represents astronomy, astrology, and space, and can stand for older women, particularly those in authority. It can also represent timing in general.

Possible Meanings in Different Types of Readings

Love: Fated relationships. Past-life connections resurface in this life, though they may be temporary.

Money: Timing is crucial. Pay attention to cycles, bills coming due, and changes in investments.

Career: Favorable for any job pertaining to space, stars, and prediction of cycles, such as stock market timing, investment counselors, and counseling in general, though not on an individual level. Psychology. On the job, immediate superiors may not have the answers. In dealing with problems, go to the top whenever possible.

Family: Older generations are active in family life. Seek the advice of elders. Bring together diverse members of the family. Live together in tight quarters. Childbirth and multiple births.

Health: Pay attention to astrology to determine effects on health. Reproductive disorders will eventually be solved.

Spiritual Path: Knowledge of the stars and astrology. Otherworld contacts, extraterrestrial and cosmic energies.

Types This Scarab Can Represent: Older women, distant authorities, the CEO emeritus of a company, people who have retired but still exert influence on a company or community.

Timing: The fifteenth day of the month or of the lunar cycle.

Location: Celestial. The Milky Way, stars in the sky, the sky itself.

16. KHEPERA

Lord of becomings, the one who becomes. In Egyptian, *kheper* is one of the most resonant root words, with many layers and shades of meaning. It means to become, to make, to create. *Kheperu* means form, manifestation, shape, image, change, and transformation. Presently living men and women were referred to as *kheperu* to distinguish them from future generations. *Kheper* could represent the spring equinox and spring itself. *Kheprit* was a goddess of the eighth hour of the day. In pre-dynastic Egypt, *Khepra* was the early beetle-headed deity of the sun, eventually moved aside by Ra. In some images, the beetle-formed Khepra is raising the sun disk into the sky, and in others, he rides the solar disk himself.

The many positive meanings associated with scarabs made the physical bugs a popular ingredient in magical spells. In some parts of Africa today, the dried scarab is added to fertility potions.

This scarab can indicate divine intervention on the matter at hand, and can indicate that the reader is on track with his or her instincts and should proceed. A visit from the great-grandfather of the gods, Khepera, is almost always positive.

Possible Meanings in Different Types of Readings

Love: Benevolent for existing relationships. Not a particularly good sign for beginning new alliances.

Money: General abundance. Inheritances. Stored resources becoming available.

Career: Favorable for jobs in aviation, solar power, manufacturing, and ceramics. Good time to ask for promotions, advancements, and new assignments.

Family: Issues dealing with previous generations and family history.

Health: Health improves or remains good. Exercise outdoors, in sunlight.

Spiritual Path: Khepera is also associated with midnight, as the sun sails through Nut's body, and with the rites performed for the gods at that time. In this form, this scarab can also be a messenger of initiation and of receiving concealed or protected knowledge.

Types This Scarab Can Represent: Grandfathers. Elder male relatives. Can also represent older men in general.

Timing: The sixteenth day of the month or of the lunar cycle.

Location: Flight, air travel, sunny places.

17. The Sistrum of Hathor

The sistrum is a symbol of Isis and especially of Isis-Hathor, goddess of love and pleasure. Hathor is the mother of the hawk god Horus in some legends, and her name means "House of Horus." Music was crucial in Hathor's rituals and many women served as musician-priestesses for her. Her major temple complex of Dendera was built in Graeco-Roman times, and still stands as a remarkable and beautiful temple. Groups of Hathor goddesses were protective deities similar to good fairies in European folktales, presiding over births and names. Their names are poetic: Lady of the Universe, Sky Storm, You from the Land of Silence, Lady of the House of Jubilation. Isis and Hathor often bear the same attributes and, on occasion, are represented in the same panel in absolutely identical attire, distinguishable only by their hieroglyphic inscriptions.

In pre-dynastic times, the sistrum was the symbol of Bat, an earlier cow-headed goddess who was worshipped in the region called the Mansion of the Sistrum. She was also called the Lady of the Two Faces, an allusion to the pair of images attached to the sistrum handle.

The sistrum is a sign of religious observation and also of music, dance, joy, and lovemaking. The sound itself is an offering, and it is cleansing energetically as well. This scarab can be positive in both romantic and health readings. However, for a sistrum to be of use, it must be shaken into activity. The presence of this scarab may exhort you to take action, break free, and embrace joy.

For those attuned to the Hathor energy, this scarab can also indicate that the reader is fulfilling or interacting with the Hathor mythos. Her scarab can also symbolize young women and loving, beautiful women of all ages.

Possible Meanings in Different Types of Readings

Love: Passionate romances. Joy. Sacred sexuality and spiritual enlightenment through love.

Money: Using money to make money. Investments.

Career: Taking action to improve situations. Shakeups at work. New colleagues, managers, opportunities. Music and dance, careers in the arts, being onstage.

Family: Active but happy time. School activities and sports.

Health: Usually this scarab indicates great energy and physical fitness in all senses. But negatives can be sexual diseases, overindulgence in food or drink, or indicate a need for exercise.

Spiritual Path: Heart-centered paths. Finding the spiritual within the physical and material world. Growing spiritually through relationships with others.

Types This Scarab Can Represent: Girls, young women, women in general, red-headed women, dancers.

Timing: The seventeenth day of the month or of the lunar cycle.

Location: Resorts, cities with active arts scenes and festivals (New Orleans, New York, Rio, Venice).

18. ANUPU THE JACKAL

Anupu, or Anubis, is the great jackal-headed guide not only of the dead but also of the astrally projecting, dreaming, and those who are on the threshold of initiation with the attendant deathlike experiences. Anubis, in the most common myth, was the son of Nephthys and Osiris, the product of their illicit liaison that Nephthys engineered by adorning herself in the guise of Isis. Abandoned by a panic-stricken Nephthys, who saw in the dog-headed babe a deformed reminder of her love for Osiris, Anubis was found by Isis, who kept him with her. He assisted Isis in finding the parts of Osiris and in the painstaking wrapping and embalming of them. In the afterlife, he weighs the soul against the feather of Maat.

Anupu's presence in a reading for health is ambivalent; he may guide you to a cure during sleep or he may guide the soul into and through the underworld, perhaps to return to the world of the living, perhaps not.

This scarab is an alert to pay attention to dream content, or to actively invoke the help of dreams in approaching a problem. Anupu, as a deity force, indicates to those in resonance with him that they may be performing or interacting with the mythos of Anubis. He leads one to new knowledge and is a strong protective force, both in the body and in the spirit. Leave this scarab in a special place inside your house to protect your home.

Possible Meanings in Different Types of Readings

Love: If outside a relationship, look to your dreams to find your partner. Dream locales may presage where you will meet in real life. Pay heed to your subconscious beliefs and desires. May indicate that the relationship is in fact initiatory rather than strictly or only romantic.

Money: Safe investments. Inheritances and loans from relatives.

Career: Skilled work, including work in the medical profession, especially anesthesiologists or surgeons. Can also indicate work in the coroner's office as an undertaker, or in hospice care situations or any setting where death and dying is a part of the job. Meticulous care in whatever profession is pursued. Can indicate exploration of new opportunities and resources.

Family: Children raised with foster families. Bright but careful children who may take more time than others. Small families, single children.

Health: Pay attention to dream content for clues to avoid illness or treat existing problems. Reproductive challenges.

Spiritual Path: Exploration of the subconscious. Hypnosis. Shamanic and underworld journeys.

Types This Scarab Can Represent: Physically or emotionally challenged children. Spiritual guides, physical teachers, and force, both in the body and in the spirit. Can also represent canine companions.

Timing: The eighteenth day of the month or of the lunar cycle.

Location: Desert, wastelands, plains, grasslands, graveyards, ancient sites with tombs, border regions.

19. Horus the Falcon

Horus is a complex deity embracing many aspects. He is probably most easily approached as Horus the Child, Her-sa-Ast, the sacred offspring of Isis and Osiris. Another aspect, the Elder Horus, is warlike, in constant and equally matched conflict with his dangerous brother Set. Originally, Horus was not considered the offspring of Isis and Osiris at all. Even the Egyptians were confused about the mythological meanderings of Horus, and their writings treat the Elder Horus and Younger Horus both as separate deities and as a combined entity.

Horus' predominant symbol is the peregrine falcon, a high-flying, circling bird of prey and strong solar symbol. The feather markings around the falcon's eye were the inspiration for the Eye of Horus symbol. Horus is generally shown as a hawk-headed deity, a bird of prey who strikes swiftly and precisely.

Horus is also the reborn or reincarnated Osiris and contains within himself the dynamic aspects of Osiris and the potential for the underworld aspects. Where Osiris represents the deceased, deified pharaoh, Horus represents the newly enthroned, living ruler.

In readings dealing with conflicts, particularly those over property or career, this scarab indicates eventual but hard-fought triumph. He is a positive force in health readings.

Possible Meanings in Different Types of Readings

Love: Attractiveness to the opposite sex. Satisfying relationships.

Money: Present lean beginnings followed by abundance. Loans from relatives may materialize.

Career: Battles for recognition. Leadership of workgroups, management in general. Legal and military employment. Best in startup companies and where competition is active. Family businesses.

Family: Problems over inheritances, possessions, or just squabbles over who gets what seat in the car.

Health: Good health in general; vigor. Sometimes can indicate eye problems, injuries from fights or sports, but generally easy recovery. Childhood diseases and disorders.

Spiritual Path: Active spiritual pursuits that do not isolate from the world. Martial arts. Activism on behalf of spiritual organizations.

Types This Scarab Can Represent: Men in general. Individuals in the military. Horus can represent a lover in romantic readings. He can also, because of his role as divine child, represent children and the concerns relating to children. He can represent young men.

Timing: The nineteenth day of the month or of the lunar cycle.

Location: Mountains, peaks, seaside cliffs, high-altitude areas.

20. Wadjet the Cobra

Wadjet the Cobra symbolizes divine action and intervention, and she presides over the marshy delta land of Lower Egypt. Cobras and snakes in general have always been both revered and feared in Egypt. One early way of writing the name of a goddess includes a cobra as a mark of divinity. Both Isis and Osiris are sometimes depicted as crowned cobras.

Cobra venom may have been employed in initiatory rites, and may also have been used by the pharaohs to perform their transition into the afterlife. Wadjet represents the burning power of kundalini, the Eye of Ra, which was also personified by Hathor and Sekhmet.

This scarab can mean that an apparently negative action must be taken to restore order. It can also indicate sudden change and activity, particularly when such changes lead to greater personal knowledge and wisdom.

Possible Meanings in Different Types of Readings

Love: Love at first sight. Abrupt, quick relationships. Romances that may not last, but may bring initiation in various forms. Learning experiences.

Money: Sudden change for good or bad. Unexpected expenses.

Career: This scarab can indicate temporary jobs, sudden "battle-field" promotions, or jobs about to end. Expect problems to erupt at work, but they may then subside. Wait and see.

Family: Short tempers and hotheadedness. Need to set and respect boundaries.

Health: Poisonings; diseases from overindulgence; substance abuse; fevers and wounds. Spinal difficulties that ultimately are healed. Chiropractic care, spinal stretching to maintain health.

Spiritual Path: As a symbol of the kundalini force, the cobra can call attention to sacred sexuality and the pursuit of enlightenment. Yoga. Wisdom teachings and explorations of ancient mysteries. Sacred dancing.

Types This Scarab Can Represent: Potent, fiery, or irritable individuals of both sexes.

Timing: The twentieth day of the month or of the lunar cycle.

Location: Jungle, grasslands, wilderness, river deltas, marshes.

21. THE SOLAR BARQUE OF RA

This scarab symbolizes the energy of the sun and the powers of Amon-Ra, who is considered in some myth cycles to be chief of the gods and, as such, a symbol—as all gods and goddesses are—of the Oneness behind the millions of deities perceived by humanity. Ra was the solar divinity, leader and creator of the other gods, personifying the solar disk. Each day his day-barque would sail across the sky and then, at dusk, be swallowed by Nut, sailing as the night-barque through her body until dawn, when the day-barque would emerge from her loins and the cycle would begin anew.

This scarab gives both complex spiritual information as well as mundane day-to-day prognostication. The rising of the sun is a cause for joy and hope, and its setting is reason for fear and distrust. This fundamental duality pervades earth-based consciousness, but both phases of the solar cycle can be regarded positively. "Night people," in particular, regard the cycles very differently than those who are up before dawn and asleep soon after dusk.

As a vessel, the Solar Barque of Ra can also indicate travel. Though indicative of change, it is benevolent.

Possible Meanings in Different Types of Readings

Love: Neutral on the subject of love. Outcome is in the hands of the questioner—nothing is resolved yet.

Money: Success in business and general financial abundance.

Career: Ups and downs. Being the rising star in a company or being downsized, possibly in a short period of time. Public events. Assisting those in authority.

Family: Indifference to issues can cause conflicts. Lack of attention to needs causes frustration. Children deceive parents, or take their own power, as in adolescence—learning to drive, going away to school, and other transitions into adulthood and independence.

Health: Good health in general. Problems related to lack or over-abundance of sunlight.

Spiritual Path: Serving the Light. Following the paths of ancient Egypt.

Types This Scarab Can Represent: Charismatic individuals, celebrities, stars of any description. This symbol of Ra can represent all those in authority, such as employers, particularly those who own or lead a company, and parents.

Timing: The twenty-first day of the month or of the lunar cycle.

Location: Sea and river travel, air travel, ships and boats, docks, harbors, sunny locations, deserts in winter.

22. Feather of Maat

Maat is the personification of justice, rightful action, and of being in accord spiritually, a complex and essential concept of Egyptian civilization. Her symbol is the Feather of Truth, against which the hearts of the deceased were weighed in the judgment hall of the afterlife. A "light" heart would balance with the feather, indicating that the soul was free of guilt. The "heavy" hearts and their possessors were fed to the hungry monster Ammit. Even the gods and goddesses would offer small statues of Maat to each other, a symbolic form of their own clear-heartedness.

A useful metaphor for understanding Maat is to consider whether an action was clear-hearted or not. If this is truly so, then the doer has nothing to fear. The laws of Maat were guidelines to check against the actions of the soul, and included concepts of truthfulness, responsibility, and humility, among others.

In readings, the symbol of Maat is a tricky one. It represents cosmic rightness, though even when we believe ourselves to be in the right, Maat may not be in accord with this idea. Before rejoicing that "right will prevail," be very sure that your position is the clear-hearted one.

Possible Meanings in Different Types of Readings

Love: Right relationships in accord with cosmic law. Clear-heartedness toward partners. Clarification of feelings.

Money: Balanced finances, sufficient money to go around, being paid what you deserve (for better or worse).

Career: Law, law enforcement, government (all in their brightest and best aspects). Social work and rehabilitation. In conflicts over finances, employment, or legal issues, right will prevail—but this may not be the "right" one expects.

Family: Balance in all things. Just discipline and reinforcement of positive traits.

Health: Adhere to proper diet and other health practices. Nothing in excess. There will be no progress without getting to underlying causes, not just treating symptoms. The natural unfolding of life, including, sometimes, its end. Heart problems.

Spiritual Path: Be clear-hearted in all your studies and practices. Strive to be balanced and avoid extremes of any kind. Chakra work, purification, yoga.

Types This Scarab Can Represent: Generally will not represent a human individual. In some cases, a judge or a lawyer who is truly fair and unbiased.

Timing: The twenty-second day of the month or of the lunar cycle.

Location: Everywhere.

23. The Pyramids

The Pyramids represent aspiration, stability, and the slow passage of time. The Pyramids also hint at mysteries concealed in the mundane casing of the outer world. It usually indicates that an event will be long in coming or long in duration. We are used to seeing the pyramids in their ruined forms. Originally, some were glazed with crushed white gypsum and inscribed with hieroglyphs, then crowned with golden capstones that glowed in the sunlight. As such, in their ruined state, they also are beacons back to older, more golden times.

Some believe that the many pyramids of Egypt are attempts to re-create the layout of the constellations in the sky. While the pyramids at Giza are best known, there are dozens of other pyramids, mostly in ruins, stretching throughout Egypt. The shape of the pyramid is a sigil for the element of fire. The elongated cousin of the pyramid, the obelisk, symbolized a solidified ray of the sun.

In a reading this scarab can indicate a need to turn back to the past, to restore, re-examine, or re-experience our formative experiences, our foundations. On a more mundane level, they can indicate building, construction, renovation, house repair, and similar activities.

Possible Meanings in Different Types of Readings

Love: The Pyramids scarab indicates relationships that build slowly, and long-term unions. It can also indicate the reappearance of people from the past, sometimes apparently from other lives, and enduring partnerships.

Money: With the Pyramids, stability is the keyword. Salaries won't rise or fall. Long-term investments are favored.

Career: Long-term employment with stable companies. Steady resources.

Family: Solid family unity. Awareness of past ancestors. Building and repairing homes and houses.

Health: Look to root causes of disease, if present. Indicates maintenance of health conditions, whether good or bad. Teeth and dental procedures.

Spiritual Path: Ancient mysteries, alternative theories of spirituality, lost civilizations, otherwordly explorations.

Types This Scarab Can Represent: Generally will not represent a human individual. Can, however, represent buildings, houses, and issues related to construction, and well-established organizations, charities, even governments.

Timing: The twenty-third day of the month or of the lunar cycle.

Location: Egypt, Mexico, mountains in all nations.

24. The Union of Isis and Osiris

This scarab indicates the essential polarity between Isis and Osiris and implies all aspects of union, from the physical to the alchemical and divine unions. It is a scarab of culmination and balance in a dynamic, not a static, form. Isis and Osiris are virtually unique among divine couples because they truly love each other. They don't bicker; they are the archetype of divine happiness in marriage. They are said to have fallen in love while still in the womb of Nut, and even to have conceived Horus while as yet unborn, or at least unmanifest in the physical world. Some say that they were not meant for each other and that Isis, as eldest daughter, was meant to marry Set, as eldest son. In this scenario, Osiris was meant to marry Nephthys, who also loved him dearly, and this mismatch was at the bottom of the conflict between Set and Osiris. So Isis and Osiris can also represent forbidden yet destined love.

Together, Isis and Osiris expressed their love for each other through strengthening and defining the civilization of Egypt. They abolished cannibalism, established laws, taught virtually every human skill and art, and provided a constant example of a union that worked.

This scarab is sacred love in all its forms and creative power at its most primal.

Possible Meanings in Different Types of Readings

Love: Marriage or committed relationships. Soul mates. Perfect unions. Good sexual relations.

Money: Powerful unions and partnerships. Shared finances.

Career: The Union scarab indicates that teamwork brings rewards; it may point to opportunities in organizing with other employees. It also is good for shared-authority situations, job splitting, and business partnerships.

Family: Usually, this scarab indicates a loving family life. Any problems are likely to be imposed from the outside.

Health: Positive indication of balanced energy. Sexual potency.

Spiritual Path: Duality, polarity, energy exchanges. Sacred sexuality, tantra, the balancing of yin and yang.

Types This Scarab Can Represent: Married or committed couples, partners in all areas of life.

Timing: The twenty-fourth day of the month or of the lunar cycle.

Location: Romantic hideaways, retreats, cruises.

25. HEQET THE FROG

Heqet, the frog goddess, is a symbol of fertility, birth, and magic. She was believed to accelerate the final stages of labor, easing birth. She had a temple at Qus in Upper Egypt, where she was mated with a form of Horus. In the Pyramid Texts, Heqet helps the king rise into the sky. Frogs appeared before the rise of the Nile, presaging the coming floods with their ribbeting calls, and were considered lucky for this reason. As a magical goddess, Heqet's name contains the word *heka*, or "magic." Some say that the modern word "hex" comes from *heka* and *heqet*, though her magical associations in ancient Egypt were uniformly positive.

Also associated with Hathor, Heqet is generally positive in health and romantic readings.

Possible Meanings in Different Types of Readings

Love: Happiness. Active emotions and sexuality. Sudden positive change.

Money: The frogs come suddenly when water returns. The Heqet scarab brings sudden windfalls, extra or merit raises, or funds from an unexpected source.

Career: Increased job satisfaction. New employment, if sought, usually at an increase in wages and benefits and without a long job search.

Family: The Heqet scarab indicates a busy family life, with many activities and lots of people around. On every block there is usually one house where all the kids gather, neighbors drop by, and relatives come to visit—that's the Heqet house. Sometimes generates too much activity for true peace of mind, but most of the time, it's too busy to notice.

Health: The Heqet scarab indicates fertility and easy childbirth. Quick resolutions to problems followed by strong overall health. Reproductive systems.

Spiritual Path: Magic. Folk spells. Midwifery. Wicca-type paths. Oracles and divination.

Types This Scarab Can Represent: Women with many children, groups.

Timing: The twenty-fifth day of the month or of the lunar cycle.

Location: Moist places, rivers, jungles, rainforests, villages, small towns.

26. MIN

Min is an early deity, whose most primitive statues may date to pre-dynastic times. He was already revered by the time of King Scorpion of the First Dynasty. In early times he was combined with Horus as the divinity "Min-Horus of the hill countries," alluding to his special patronage of the mining country of Egypt. He could be seen as the son of Isis, or she could be seen as his consort, producing the child Horus. While Osiris' phallus was ultimately lost, Min's was ever-present.

Though some apologists try to de-emphasize or disguise his sexuality, the Egyptians delighted in him for his potency. In the Coffin Texts, deceased males call on Min as an example for their own post-death sexual powers. In Plutarch's version of the story of Isis and Osiris, Isis was at Coptos (modern Qift, Min's sacred city) when news of the attack on Osiris reached her, whereupon she immediately cut off a lock of her hair. Hair had sexual connotations in Egypt; to be found with one's hair disordered meant that a woman was sexually willing or vulnerable.

The Greeks saw in Min a counterpart of their god Pan. He was seen as the guardian of desert travelers, as the trading caravans started out from his city. Even after the decline of Egypt, Qift remained a vibrant and successful city. Perhaps Min's patronage continued.

Powerful god of maleness, masculinity, sexuality, and sensuality, the presence of this scarab in a reading indicates vigor in all areas.

Possible Meanings in Different Types of Readings

Love: May indicate that an attraction is primarily sexual rather than emotional. Quick, intense involvements.

Money: Expanding abundance. Good returns on investments, especially mining, metals, and gems.

Career: New challenges easily met at work.

Family: Adolescence and attendant hormones. Sporting activities and general energy in all areas of family life.

Health: Healing of sexual, reproductive, and urinary problems. General vigor.

Spiritual Path: Assertiveness and power over pleasure. Tantric explorations. Conquest of sexuality through experiencing it rather than denying it.

Types This Scarab Can Represent: Virile men, often unmarried. A man in the prime of his life.

Timing: The twenty-sixth day of the month or of the lunar cycle.

Location: Mountains, deserts, hub cities, places where trade and commerce are carried out, convention centers, and resorts.

27. The Ushabti

Ushabti or shabti figures are small faience images placed in tombs to answer for the dead if they were called upon to work in the fields of the Duat, or Netherworld. They were substitute versions of the tomb's owner, who would do the labor otherwise required of him or her. The earliest ushabtis date to burials around 2100 B.C.E. and are nude, crude forms made of wax, mud, wood, or dough, hardly the sophisticated and artistic figures that became common later. Some burials include 365 ushabtis, apparently one for each day of the year, occasionally with extra "overseer" ushabtis to help supervise the gang. The late-period pharaoh Taharqa took no chances: he had more than a thousand of them in his tomb. Wealthy individuals had their own ushabtis made with their names inscribed in the clay, but most people could only afford "generic" ushabtis that had blank spaces for adding their names in ink at the time of burial.

Originally, the ushabti figures were made out of persea tree wood, a relative of the avocado, and a tree that is sacred to Isis. Early ushabtis were bare of writing, but later ones had a band of hieroglyphics around the waist, forming a binding spell that forced the figure to answer for the tomb owner if any work was required of him or her in the underworld. Some of the figures have inscriptions indicating that their chief task was to carry sand from one side of the Nile to the other, and back again. Perhaps it was this specific kind of busy work that they were meant to preserve their owner from, or a type of nearly impossible magical task that had to be fulfilled, like the Greek labors of Hercules or the fairy tale of spinning straw into gold. Or it may have simply been a magical method of keeping the tomb clear of sand, also a nearly impossible task.

Possible Meanings in Different Types of Readings

Love: The Ushabti scarab can indicate undue dependency on another, or exploitation of someone less experienced in matters of the heart. It can also mean outside helpers, good or bad, involved in a relationship.

Money: Seek advice on investments and employment.

Career: This scarab often indicates the hiring of new employees. It is a good time for job seekers. It may mean a pick-up in business that requires additional help. Expect to be supervising new or inexperienced workers, or be one of them yourself.

Family: Seek advice. Family meetings. Delegation. Indicates unexpected or even unwarranted assistance from friends or family, even after a long breach in the relationship.

Health: This scarab can mean a period of being unable to be very active and of wishing to or being forced to rely on the help of others. Also refers to medical assistants, nurses, and all those who assist in healing.

Spiritual Path: This scarab can indicate someone who is just beginning on the spiritual path, and who needs guidance to get off to a good start. Study with a spiritual teacher, assist others in a charity or religious group environment, and seek advice from those who have experience in a given area.

Types This Scarab Can Represent: Assistants, trainees, helpers, children. Employees and helpful persons of either gender, usually but not always young. Ushabti figures represent souls in a less-developed state of evolution, or in the process of self-transformation that is not yet complete. The Ushabti symbol can also be seen as the pupal stage of the Khepra beetle's development.

Timing: The twenty-seventh day of the month or of the lunar cycle.

Location: No specific location.

28. The Incense Bowl

The incense bowl filled with grains of fragrant resin was a common offering to deities, offered even by the pharaoh and his queen, or by the gods, to each other. Sometimes, instead of a bowl, a small model of the human arm would be extended toward the god or goddess, holding a sweetly smoking cup of incense.

Incense was vital to Egyptian temple practices, and its trade was important. Hatshepsut's expedition to Punt brought back incense trees to be planted in the sacred gardens, which she announced as proudly as other pharaohs had trumpeted their successes in battle.

One of the most commonly used incenses was myrrh, sacred to Ra and to Isis. It was also used as a magical ink, mouthwash, and even as snuff. *Kyphi*, a mixture of wine, resins, and other ingredients, was also used in the temples, especially at night.

The presence of the Incense Bowl scarab in a reading indicates that it is necessary to pay attention to the spiritual and to communication with your deities, and to make offerings of time and thought. You may find it necessary to make offerings to others in your life to maintain or restore harmony. Routine will be comforting—try to avoid drastic changes during this time.

Possible Meanings in Different Types of Readings

Love: As an offering item, the presence of the Incense Bowl scarab advises to avoid selfishness, and to focus on giving in order to receive.

Money: It is a good time to spend money on repairs and give to charity. Share the wealth.

Career: Consistent work over a long period leads to benefits and promotions.

Family: Expect closeness in the family unit and group activities, especially charitable ones.

Health: The Incense Bowl pertains to stones, tumors, swellings, and fevers. To maintain health, make consistent offerings to yourself by following a daily regime of proper diet and exercise.

Spiritual Path: Compassionate work for others, volunteering, offering one's own skills and talents.

Types This Scarab Can Represent: This scarab can represent someone who is in service to another, or who is dedicated to a life of service to humanity or to a religious faith.

Timing: The twenty-eighth day of the month or of the lunar cycle.

Location: Natural preserves, parks, forests, religious buildings.

29. THE SPHINX

The Sphinx, an enigmatical human-headed lion lying on the desert, concealing its age and true origins, has been a symbol of mystery for thousands of years. Even modern researchers can't agree on its age and origins, and the mystic Edgar Cayce predicted a mysterious chamber underneath filled with arcane secrets and records. Chambers have recently been discovered beneath the Sphinx, but what they contain remains a mystery. Was it originally a gigantic statue of lion-maned Sekhmet? Some experts believe that the head of the Sphinx is too small for its body, indicating extensive remodeling at some point in its history. Presently, its age is the subject of sharp debate between conservative Egyptologists and new theorists who believe it is many thousands of years older than the accepted chronology allows. But the Sphinx has always been a beast of mystery, communicating in a dream to one future pharaoh, asking to be swept clean of sand. He obliged, and subsequently ascended the throne.

The original riddle of the Sphinx was said to be "What walks on four legs in the morning, two at noon, and three at evening?" The answer was humanity—crawling as a baby, walking on two legs as an adult, and assisted by a cane in old age. The Sphinx here asks another question—"Do you know the question you *should* be asking?" A deeper look inside may be necessary.

For the Greeks, the Sphinx was the symbol of ultimate knowledge, of wisdom more ancient than time itself. Crowned with the sacred cobra, it combines the royal energies of the pharaoh and two of the potent, dangerous Eyes of Ra—Sekhmet and Uadjet. Letting sleeping dogs lie is good advice—and it applies even more to sleeping, or merely resting, lions.

In a reading, it can mean that no answer is available or revealable at this time . . . or that you're asking the wrong question.

Possible Meanings in Different Types of Readings

Love: As a symbol of ancient times, the Sphinx can show that lovers have been involved before, and may be working out a destiny between the two of them. Secrets from the past may influence present relationships. Generally, the Sphinx in love readings indicates steady and enduring relationships.

Money: In money and material matters, the Sphinx is positive for the very long term, negative or neutral for the short term. It is favorable for building and real estate as long as quick gains are not sought.

Career: The Sphinx usually provides a stabilizing influence at work. Job situations continue. It is a good portent for reaching the top of your profession, whatever that is, and staying there. But are you doing what you really should be doing?

Family: Look for secrets from the past affecting the present.

Health: The Sphinx usually indicates no changes, at least no quick ones. It can suggest long convalescences and illnesses related to stagnant energy or lack of activity. This can change if the active aspects of the Sphinx energy can be brought into play, as both Sekhmet and Uadjet are powerful healers.

Spiritual Path: Ancient knowledge, past lives affecting the current life, clearing of childhood experiences. Delving deep to retrieve information. Trance work. Energy work.

Types This Scarab Can Represent: This scarab can represent an elderly person of either gender.

Timing: The twenty-ninth day of the month or of the lunar cycle.

Location: Isolated rock outcroppings, hills.

30. Serqet the Scorpion

Scorpions were abundant in ancient Egypt, and several potentially deadly varieties stalked the lands along the Nile, in the desert, and in the swamps of the delta. The sudden pain and even death that these small creatures could bring was seen as dangerous, and so potent that it must be divine. One of the first kings took the name Scorpion, and the goddess Serqet earned reverence from early times.

Scorpions were also associated with Isis. When fleeing from Set, Isis was accompanied by a bodyguard of seven scorpions, led by Tefen, who protected Isis and attacked anyone who stood against her. When a wealthy, arrogant woman turned away Isis when she asked for shelter, the scorpions pooled their poison, killed her son, and set her house on fire. Isis, horrified, restored the boy to life and put out the fire with a rainstorm. When her own son was stung by a scorpion, this time sent by Set, Isis succeeded in obtaining special healing spells for him and restored him to life. Serqet may appear with the headdress of Isis. Along with Neith and Nephthys, Isis and Serqet stood guard around the inner golden shrine of Tutankhamen.

The image of the scorpion was used on amulets, including scarabs, to protect against scorpion bite and, by extension, all types of sudden, unexpected attack.

In nature, scorpions are not all bad. Unlike most insects, scorpions care for their young, carrying them around on their backs, and even "nursing" them, feeding them directly through the skin where they cling to their mother.

Possible Meanings in Different Types of Readings

Love: The scorpion strikes abruptly and indicates sudden change, strong sexual relationships, and disruptions from a new person affecting existing relationships. The scorpion sting can strike like Cupid's arrow.

Money: Again, as in love, the Serqet scarab speaks of sudden change in finances, either up or down, depending on nearby scarabs in a reading. On the plus side, this can represent infusions of capital.

Career: This scarab is favorable for work in medical research. It can also be good for work in security, or in any field where protecting others is a part of it, such as childcare. In most cases, success will be in a group atmosphere, working with others rather than independently.

Family: In myth, the scorpion Tefen led her six scorpion sisters to assist Isis, unfortunately interpreting this assistance to include attacking a woman who denied Isis shelter. The Scorpion scarab indicates cooperative family efforts, though these may be misguided. It also represents strong yet nurturing mothers, and large families.

Health: Sudden changes, either for good or ill. Illness may call for drastic therapies. Beware of insect bites, food poisoning, and fevers.

Spiritual Path: The Serqet scarab favors exploring spirituality through the healing arts and by protecting others. It can indicate that the will needs to be strengthened, but also controlled.

Types This Scarab Can Represent: Independent women given to sudden, decisive action.

Timing: Represents the thirtieth day of the month or the fractional portion of the thirtieth day of the lunar cycle.

Location: Wilderness, deserts, mountains, swamps.

CREATING
SCARAB AMULETS

E gyptian magicians, often scribes trained in sacred writings of all kinds at the House of Life, drew inscriptions on metal foils to use as amulets. The local magician or priest would inscribe the sacred hiero-glyphs using a burin or similar tool, and then, with the appropriate words of power, fold or roll the metal sheet around a string for wearing. Several of the divination scarabs can be used to make similar impressions, which can be folded up and inserted into a locket, slipped into a medicine bag, or simply carried in a pocket or purse.

Of course, you can also carry the actual scarabs, rather than just their impressions, but if you want to keep the set together, this is an easy, alternative way of keeping their energies with you.

MAKING AN IMPRESSION
OF A SCARAB

Select the scarab you wish to copy. Lay a piece of tin foil or aluminum foil over the back of the scarab (paper-backed foils, such as the ones used in craft projects, will also work). Simply running over the foil with your finger will produce an image. Once in, the impression on the foil is almost impossible to completely erase. You can also use a ballpoint pen to inscribe the symbol on the foil.

If you are working within a system or tradition, set up a sacred space accordingly. If not, simply arrange together pleasing items related to the symbol on the scarab. The preparing of sacred space is a way of focusing on the preparation of the amulet, and can increase its effects for you. However, simply carrying the symbol will also bring those energies to you, though you won't be as keenly aware of them as you would be if you go through a ritual experience in preparing the amulet.

Generally, only one amulet should be carried at a time. If this doesn't seem to be enough, examine your life carefully to see where you need to make changes rather than rely on the energy symbolized by the amulet.

MEANINGS OF THE SCARABS
FOR FOIL AMULETS

1. The Lotus

To bring peaceful completion to a situation.
To symbolize enlightenment.

Prepare a sacred space filled with beauty—with flowers, bowls of water, sweet incense, and images of lotuses. Inscribe the foil and say these or similar words before folding it:

> *Sushen, sacred lotus, flowering bud of Ra, cradle of Nefertum, beloved flower of Isis, bring to me peaceful resolutions and true enlightenment.*

2. Sobek the Crocodile

Protection against unseen forces.

For Sobek, prepare a sacred area with a vessel of water and an image of a crocodile or alligator. The predominant color is preferably green. Inscribe the foil, and then say something like this:

> *Sobek, Lord of the Green Plume, swift and fierce, yet patient and observant, protect me from what may be concealed.*

3. The Palm Tree

For reducing stress.

Set up images of things you find calming, including a picture of a palm or a frond or palm products, such as dates or coconuts. Take a few moments and visualize whatever brings rest and relaxation to you until you can feel the stress leaving you, or at least reducing in intensity. When you feel as relaxed as possible, make the image of the amulet and say these or words like them:

> *The palm oasis gives shade and refreshment; may I be refreshed and may all of my tasks go easily.*

Fold the foil loosely around the string if you want to wear it, or just fold it into an easy-to-carry shape. For this amulet, the foil should not be tightly compressed and should be loose enough to unfold if desired.

4. The Throne of Isis

To bring the wisdom, protection, and attention
of this mighty goddess into your life.

Arrange an altar with an image of Isis that you like, adding a pleasant, sweet incense and candles if you wish. Inscribe or impress the scarab onto the foil, and say these or similar words:

> Hail Isis, Ast, Goddess of the Universe, Mistress of the All, look on me as you looked on your son Horus; protect me with tender care and love. Keep me from pain and guide me to enlightenment. As I carry this amulet, may I always be aware of you, and may you always be aware of me. Great Isis, I thank you.

5. Crook and Flail of Osiris

To cause a situation to be wisely resolved.

Select an image of Osiris. Isis may also be included. Say:

> Osiris, Ausar, Lord of the Underworld, wise ruler of Egypt on earth, may all things be resolved with wisdom and compassion. Let all pettiness and dissension be dissolved in all those concerned in this matter. May your wisdom and judgment prevail. Hail, Osiris!

6. Seshat, Lady of Writing

To inspire written projects, reports, and all things
to do with books, writing, and writers. Also for
blessings on the modern equivalent of the scribe:
the secretary, librarian, or office worker.

To make this amulet, create a sacred space in a bookcase, or surrounded by books and the implements of writing.

> *Seshat, Lady of Books, Lady of Words, Architect and Guardian*
> *of the Great House, guide me in my words and my works. Let*
> *all that I produce be accurate, graceful, and truthful. Praise to*
> *Seshat, Goddess of the Word.*

7. The Shen

To keep things as they are.

Draw the image of the shen on a piece of paper. This is an abstract concept, not a deity, so you are bringing its symbolic power into the scarab amulet. Nekhebet, the vulture goddess often shown clutching the shen in her talons, may also be invoked as the divine protectress of the status quo.

> *May that which continues, continue. May what is going on,*
> *go on. May the cycles persist, again and again and again,*
> *round as the shen, bound as the shen.*

8. Tahuti the Ibis

To invoke wisdom and assist on tests.

The ibis is black and white, like the moon phases of which Thoth is also master. Use these colors in a sacred space, adding an image of Thoth or the ibis.

> *Lord of Wisdom, Tahuti, great, great, great,*
> *Let my mind be as clear and encompassing as yours;*
> *May I forget nothing that I should remember*
> *May my knowledge be sufficient for any question,*
> *Tahuti thrice-great, guide me, wise one!*

9. Bast the Cat

To bring joy to the bearer.

Red and green are Bast's colors. Incorporate them into a sacred area, adding a Bast or any cat image. Toy with a necklace or a string of beads as you say the following, or similar, words:

> *Bastet, divine Cat, swift Cat, powerful Cat, sweet Cat,*
> *To whom every moment is a joyous moment, filled with pleasure!*
> *Chewing, chasing, dancing, mating,*
> *Stalking, napping, watching, eating,*
> *May all things that bring joy be in my life,*
> *May all my joys be an offering to you, Great Cat!*

10. The Ankh

To raise energy and vitality.
Good for assisting in healing.

Again, this is an abstract concept. Clear a sacred space and adorn it with Egyptian images. Call divine or universal energy into your body, then inscribe the foil.

> *Life rising, life flowing, life calling, life sowing,*
> *The energy of Life is the Energy of all things.*
> *The Energy of all things is the energy in me.*
> *The Energy of all things is the energy in my amulet.*

11. The Temple

To sanctify your environment, protect from
outside forces, and raise consciousness.

For this amulet, set up a sacred space. If you are dedicated to a specific divinity, place those objects in the sacred area. Meditate on an idealized temple beside the Nile, one that is safe, active, and perpetually alive on the inner planes. Note all you see, hear, and feel. Gather these impressions to you firmly, repeating them in your mind while you are meditating. Come away from the inner image of the temple knowing that it exists. With that energy around you, inscribe the foil with the temple gate. End the meditation and know that the temple exists and is as close as the amulet you have created—even closer, for it exists within you.

12. The Nile

**To help go with the flow, and to
ease anxiety and stress.**

If possible, go to natural flowing water, a stream, or a river, glinting in sunlight. Any of these can symbolize the mystical Nile. The Egyptians believed that the physical Nile was reflected in the stars of the Milky Way, which formed a Celestial Nile splitting the sky as the Nile bisected Egypt. If you can't reach flowing water, gather the energy of the slowly flowing stars in the night sky above.

> *Great river bringing life,*
> *Sparkling waters, sparkling stars,*
> *Never-ceasing, ever-flowing,*
> *Eternally journeying, all things come,*
> *All things pass, what troubles me, too, shall go on,*
> *Washing away with the imperishable Nile.*

Fold the amulet. Carry it with you.

13. Nephthys

To dispel fear and increase intuition.

Set up a dark-colored altar with an image of Nephthys, preferably at dusk or in the early evening. Say these or similar words:

> *Neb-het, Nepthys, Lady of Dreams,*
> *Goddess who has known fear, and has known conquest of fear,*
> *Ease my fears with insight and intuition.*

14. Set

The tricky energy of the Set scarab is not recommended as an amulet, unless one feels very in accord with both his mythos and his methods. In drastic situations this scarab could be carried for protection, but should be in the company of the Isis scarab.

15. *The Starry Sky of Nut*

To counteract negative astrological configurations,
and to get answers from those in authority.

Prepare the amulet first, inscribing the stars or pressing the foil against the scarab. Take the scarab and the foil with you, and go outside under the stars. Wear dark or shimmery clothing. If there is any light, try to catch it against the foil so that it sparkles, like a star.

> *Hail, Nut! Goddess of the starry sky!*
> *May all your stars shine benevolently upon me.*
> *May all those whose seats are in the mansions of stars*
> *Look upon me with kindness.*
> *Hail, Nut!*

16. *Khepera*

To enhance creativity and inspiration.

Decorate a sacred area with images of Khepera, or arrange the scarabs in this set in a design on the altar, perhaps creating a huge Khepera from the little scarabs. Say words like this:

> *Khepera, self-creating, self-knowing,*
> *Divine creator, who flies as he pleases,*
> *Let me share in your creative power*
> *May my skills and talents increase*
> *Under your inspiration. Hail, Khepera!*

Create the amulet either by pressing it against the scarab or inscribing the foil yourself. Fold it around a string or necklace if you want to wear it.

17. *The Sistrum of Hathor*

To change and cleanse tense situations and
replace them with happiness and love.

Set up your sacred space. If you have a sistrum or rattle, use them. If not, the word *seseshe* means "sistrum," but is also similar to the sound the sistrum imitates, the plucking of papyrus reeds. Saying it (*se-se-she* or *se-se-shuh*) is equivalent to the offering of the sistrum to Hathor. The sistrum was also used extensively in rites of Isis and Bast.

> *Seseshe, seseshe, the sistrum of Hathor,*
> *Seseshe, seseshe, the sound of laughter,*
> *Seseshe, seseshe, transforms all matter.*

Repeat until you feel cheered. Inscribe the foil, and fold it around a string.

18. Anupu the Jackal

> **For protection. Place under the pillow for guidance**
> **and protection in dreams, or keep with you**
> **while under anesthesia.**

> *Anupu, dark Lord, great guide,*
> *Lead me to find all parts of myself.*
> *Keep me safe in my journeys,*
> *On earth and in the other worlds.*

19. Horus the Falcon

> **To enhance leadership qualities and**
> **ensure protection by a strong defense.**

Prepare the foil ahead of time, if you like, or do it outside. Go outside when the sun is shining, preferably where there are falcons, hawks, or other high-flying raptors. Wait until one is visible, and then say these or similar words:

> *Horus, Sun falcon, swift flyer,*
> *Clear-eyed, bright-feathered*
> *Rightful heir who has ascended,*
> *Let me share in your qualities*
> *And triumph in your name.*

Catch the sunlight on the metal foil, then wrap it around the string.

20. Wadjet the Cobra

For protection.

Set up a sacred space with an image of Wadjet, or any Egyptian image that shows the cobra, such as the royal crown or the winged solar disk that often includes the uraeus. Say these or similar words and fold the amulet around the string.

Swift protector, Lady of Egypt, Green One of the Delta,
Defender of the throne, guardian of the temple,
Healer of ills, nurse of Horus, friend to Isis,
Protect me as tenderly, lean lady of silent movement.
Lion lady, guard me always in this image.

21. The Solar Barque of Ra

For safety in flying, sailing, and travel of all kinds.

Go outside, into the sun. Prepare the scarab beforehand and show it to the rays of the sun, or inscribe it while you are outside. Meditate on the sun's power for a few moments before saying these or similar words:

Ra, Great Lord of the Sky,
He who sails in his barque across the sky
Again and again, without error,
May all vessels that carry me, carry me as safely.
May all who greet you, greet me as warmly.
Hail, Ra! Lord of the Universe, grant my prayer.

22. Feather of Maat

For the truth to be served and true justice to prevail.
Be sure you or your cause are truly in the right
before carrying this amulet.

Take a feather, preferably white, and hold it up to an image or object symbolizing the divine to you and, especially, to the divine order underlying all things.

I offer the feather of Maat
To the Divine that is All there is.
Let the truth be served;
Let justice prevail in this matter.
May all be in accord with the
Will of the Divine.
May I be with Truth, and One with Truth.
May All be with Truth, and One with Truth.

Fold the foil carefully, making sure the image of the feather is not bent sharply.

23. The Pyramids

To stabilize shaky situations.

Include in your sacred space pictures of the pyramids or the small, souvenir models of them. Say words like these:

The pyramids are built solidly, in accord with cosmic will, and endure through all conditions. May this Pyramids amulet enable me to assist in the creation of lasting, stable conditions, and may the forces of chaos have no power. Like the pyramids, built against the earth, yet pointing to the celestial heavens, may balance and calmness endure around me and through them bring enlightenment.

Inscribe or impress the scarab against the foil, and carry it with you. It can also be placed in or underneath objects near you, which is handy in work situations.

24. The Union of Isis and Osiris

For happy relationships and marriages.

Decorate a sacred space with images of Isis and Osiris, or of any male image with any female image. Floral incenses or Egyptian kyphi are good scents for this amulet. They should be representations that you enjoy and feel comfortable about.

*True love is rare in any time and place, even among the gods
and goddesses. Isis and Osiris knew the joy of true love; let us
also know the joy of true love, which enhances the soul and
exalts the heart. Isis and Osiris were wise in the ways of love;
let us also be wise in the ways of love, knowing how to avoid
hurt and bring joy to one another. The love of Isis and Osiris
endures; let our love also endure, lasting through all tests and
troubles. May our love be an adornment to Isis and Osiris,
and may we be adornments to each other.*

This amulet will help enhance relationships; however, it will not
compel love from someone who does not feel it. It will help clear out
extraneous influences and let the two of you discover and appreciate
each other. If carried to bring a relationship, substitute "me" for "us,"
"my love" for "our love," and so on.

25. Heqet the Frog

For fertility and creativity.

Create a sacred space with bowls of water and an image of a frog or of
Heqet herself. Add flowers or plants for a green, riverside environment.

*The Nile rises, the frogs come,
Little Heqets, every one;
Abundant creation, continuing
Abundant fertility, generating
May the heka of Heqet bring
Fertilization and creation.*

26. Min

For vigor and sexual potency.

Adorn an altar or other sacred space with masculine images, including
Min if possible. Phallic symbols, such as pine cones, fruits, and other
similarly shaped objects, can also represent Min. Inscribe the amulet
as you say these or similar words:

Min, mighty Lord of Coptos,
Ever potent, ever strong,
Unfailing of desire and fulfillment of desire,
Bringer of life, freer from strife,
Min, great of power, join your power to my amulet.
Thank you, mighty one!

27. The Ushabti

For assistance from others.

Put an ushabti image in your sacred space. Draw one or more of them on the foil.

Answerers, may I have your aid,
Whenever I may need it;
May the Power of the All
Share with me the willing assistance of others
To attain my just and proper goals.

Fold the amulet and carry with you when you need help.

28. The Incense Bowl

To symbolize spiritual offerings and
remind you of spiritual service.

If you make daily offerings or prayers using incense, make this amulet at the time you perform your usual rite. Pass the scarab through the smoke.

I offer incense and I offer myself
To service of the Divine.
Let this amulet be my token,
Reminding me always of my role
In the unfolding of the universe.

29. The Sphinx

To keep quiet in difficult situations and prevent gossip.

Purify a working space, and place on it an image of the Sphinx. Say these or similar words as you make the foil amulet.

> *May I have the wisdom and the silence of the Sphinx,*
> *Keeper of mysteries. Silence is golden, like the sands of Egypt;*
> *May I keep my own counsel.*

30. Serqet the Scorpion

**For protection, particularly when in difficult
circumstances or when you are alone.**

Create a sacred space with an image of Serqet, preferably in the less hotheaded Isis-Serqet form.

> *Swift scorpion, loving mother, defending goddess,*
> *Protect me when no other protects me.*

Say seven times while folding the metal around a string.

APPENDIX I
THE EGYPTIAN
HIEROGLYPHIC ALPHABET

E gyptian scarabs are inscribed with hieroglyphics, the sacred symbols used to write the Egyptian language for religious and monu-
mental purposes. It was believed that each individual drawing possessed a special meaning, similar to the Chinese written language, and
that there was no "alphabet" as such. For many centuries, the secrets of
these enigmatical symbols were concealed, until a French researcher
named Jean François Champollion discovered that the symbols could
represent both things and sounds.

The key to the decipherment was the Rosetta Stone, a three-lan-
guage proclamation that was in Greek, the everyday demotic Egyptian
writing, and, finally, the sacred hieroglyphic script. The Greek version
was easily read, and it mentioned a Ptolemaic pharaoh and his queen,
an earlier Cleopatra. Champollion noticed that several groups of figures were contained in a semicircular chamber reminiscent of the
shape of a rifle cartridge—in French, a *cartouche.*

Champollion realized that it was likely only the royal names would
be so specially treated. He compared the contents of the cartouches

against the approximate positions in the Greek text, and discovered that these two names were those of Ptolemy and Queen Cleopatra, not the Cleopatra of later fame, but an earlier Ptolemaic queen. Examining the individual symbols in the cartouches, he realized that some were repeated. He saw that the names Cleopatra and Ptolemy also shared several letters in Greek. Champollion put it all together and discovered that the Egyptian language had many symbols that represented individual words, but it also possessed an "alphabet" by which foreign names could be spelled out, and which was also used for spelling most words in Egyptian.

The stones were no longer silent. The walls began to speak, and true Egyptology was born.

While the nuances of Egyptian language are complex enough to occupy a lifetime, the basics are simple. Here is the "secret" that Champollion discovered, the twenty-five-symbol "alphabet," plus a few alternates.

Sign	*Object*	*Pronunciation*
	Vulture	A glottal stop—for example, if you say "uh-uh," the glottal stop is what occurs between the first "uh" and the second "uh." Some times misused as an "a" vowel sound in transliteration, most notably for cartouche jewelry, but this is incorrect.
	Reed	"Yuh" in the middle of a word, "ah" sound in the beginning.

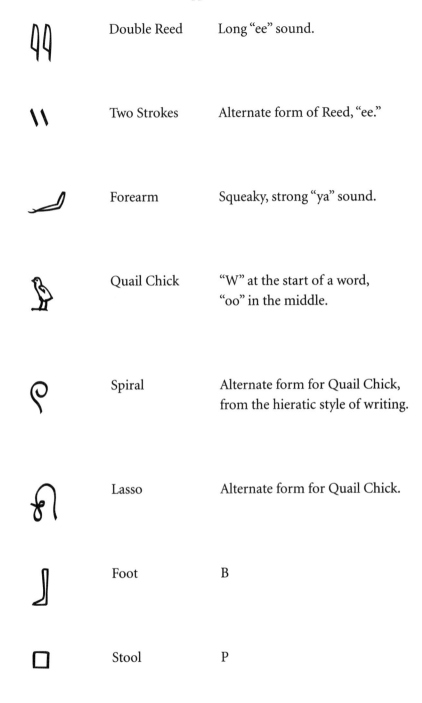

	Double Reed	Long "ee" sound.
	Two Strokes	Alternate form of Reed, "ee."
	Forearm	Squeaky, strong "ya" sound.
	Quail Chick	"W" at the start of a word, "oo" in the middle.
	Spiral	Alternate form for Quail Chick, from the hieratic style of writing.
	Lasso	Alternate form for Quail Chick.
	Foot	B
	Stool	P

Horned Viper   F

 Owl   M

 Rib   Alternate form of m.

 Water   N

 Crown   Alternate form of n.

 Mouth   R

 Lion   Alternate for r above, or l, used in writing foreign words as the "L" sound was absent in Egypt.

 House Plan   H

Twisted Wick	Emphatic h, "heh."
Placenta (?)	Voiceless "kh," a spitty, hissy sound similar to a human imitating a cat hiss.
Animal Belly	Voiced "kh," actually pronounced as a French or Spanish rolling "rr."
Door Bolt	S, or, earlier in the Old Kingdom, a z sound.
Bolt of Cloth	S.
Pool	Sh.
Hillside	Q, pronounced like the "c" in "cat."

| | Basket | K, pronounced like the "k" in "kitten." Listen closely—there is a difference from the "c" in cat. |

| | Ring Stand | G; hard g, "guh," not "juh." |

| | Loaf | T |

| | Pestle | T (alternate for the loaf). |

| | Tether | "Ch" as in church. |

| | Hand | D |

| | Cobra Snake | "Dj," "juh" sound. |

While several of the sounds are vowel-like, and are accepted as semivowels by experts, none of the symbols are true vowels. Because of this, no one knows exactly how the Egyptian language was pronounced in ancient times. The only surviving dialect of ancient Egyptian, Coptic, has had over fifteen hundred years to evolve and change, and the original sounds may not have been the most widespread or standard pronunciations. The variations in pronunciations of English often vary within parts of the same city, or, in America, from north to south and east to west. In Egyptian, *Nfr*, meaning "good" or "beautiful," could have possible pronunciations of nofer, nefer, nufer, nufor, or many others . . . or no vowel sounds at all. We just don't know, though theories abound and various experts prefer one pronunciation over another.

In addition to the basic signs above, there were many biliterals and triliterals, single or combined images, that carried a full word value of two or three sounds. Here are a few found in inscriptions and on scarabs, made pronounceable by inserting vowel sounds using "Egyptological" Egyptian:

Nesu Bity   King of Upper and Lower Egypt.

Neter Nefer   Good god, often a title of the pharaoh.

Di Ankh   Giving life.

Ankh wedja seneb — Life, prosperity, health.

 Hotep — Peace, satisfaction.

 Neb — Lord.

 Djed — Stability.

 Ka — One of the nine parts of the soul.

Here are some inscriptions from scarabs.

"May Bast grant you a Happy New Year." This formula was used with other divinities as well. Sometimes just "Happy New Year" was used. Like modern greeting cards, sometimes the sender and recipient were specified, as in:

"May Ptah give a Happy New Year, from Prince Shashanq to his Mother Ka-ra-ma-ma"

Note: scarab inscriptions often used an abbreviated or corrupt version of Egyptian, and can be hard to read. Some symbols are included solely for their magical meanings, and do not form words with adjacent symbols. Plurals were indicated by repeating signs, as in the row of "neters" below.

"Isis, Lady of Heaven, Mistress of the Gods"

"Life and Beauty"

APPENDIX II
MAKING YOUR OWN
DIVINATION SCARABS

If you want to add more scarabs to your personal set, or create a special one, there are several ways of making divination scarabs. The first, and the easiest but most expensive, is to purchase ready-made scarabs and simply draw the symbols on their flat bases or on their backs, using a Sharpie, Pilot, or similar fine-point pen. The symbol can also be drawn on adhesive paper and then cut out and attached to the flat side of the scarab. To protect the symbol, spray it with a layer of lacquer or sealant.

Scarabs are easy to form out of clay, either the modern polymer clays such as Fimo or Sculpey, or any type of ceramic material. The designs can be glazed in or added after the scarabs have been baked.

Take a small lump of clay and roll it into a ball—just like the scarabs themselves did with their egg cases. Squeeze the sides of the ball slightly, and then press the clay onto a flat surface. Adjust the shape so it is nicely oval. Take a sharp tool and inscribe a T shape on the back of the scarab. Where the two lines meet, form a tiny triangle.

This is the basic scarab shape. If you like, you can add more detail, including marks for the legs and elytra.

If you have a scarab from Egypt, you can make a mold from it. Take a lump of clay about four times bigger than the scarab you want to use to make the mold. If using polymer clay, make sure it is well conditioned (thoroughly kneaded) before making your mold. Set it aside a few moments to let it cool down and lose some of the heat it has absorbed from your hands. If it is too warm and soft, it will not capture as much detail.

Flatten the ball of clay onto a smooth surface, making sure that it is about twice as thick as the scarab whose imprint you want to take. If the scarab is pierced for stringing, run a string through the holes. This will make it easier to remove from the clay mold. Now press your scarab, curved-side down, into the clay. Press it in firmly, making sure all of the edges touch the clay. Then, carefully remove the scarab, tugging on the strings to lift it up, or using a fingernail to loosen an edge. You may have to bend the clay slightly to do this, but this won't appreciably hurt the mold. Just gently bend it back to its original shape.

Now bake the mold according to the instructions on the clay package. Once it is baked, use it to mold more scarabs. After every few scarabs, pop the mold and the clay into the freezer for a minute or two to cool them down. This will help prevent the clay from sticking to the mold. You can also sprinkle the mold with talcum powder or pulver to help assure its easy release. Bake the scarabs according to the instructions, or fire them in a kiln, following the guidelines for the type of clay.

If you decide to create a "deluxe" set of stone scarabs, these associations can help you choose which stone scarab matches what symbol. Blue or green faience clay, sometimes called "glazed composition," or glazed steatite (a type of soapstone) were common materials, and if necessary, can always be used. Silver or gold scarabs, artificially rare now due to millennia of melting for reuse, were probably used for virtually every symbol; in modern times, Egyptian silver scarabs may be less expensive than many carved stones. These are not the only possibilities but are traditional stones associated with different deities and symbols, or are logical choices based on the symbolism and meanings. The unlikely bronze as a substance for Maat scarabs is historically attested—bronze scarabs marked with her symbol were also sometimes used as scale weights.

Horus scarabs were often—one author states "exclusively"—of lapis lazuli. In some cases, if another amulet or image of a deity is known to have been depicted in a particular stone, it is suggested here for a scarab.

When using multicolored scarab sets, where repeated use may let the reader identify the symbol by just a glimpse of the scarab, it is best to draw them unseen from a pouch, or shake them out one at a time.

Lotus: faience, amethyst, jade

Sobek: faience, malachite, olivine

Palm Tree: faience, green jasper, olivine

Throne of Isis: faience, carnelian, gold, amethyst, red or yellow jasper, bloodstone

Crook and Flail: faience, gold, hematite

Seshat: white stone

Shen: faience, agate

Tahuti: faience, white or black and white stone, silver, emerald, glass

Bast: faience, green or red stones

Ankh: faience, gold, silver

Temple: faience, granite, diorite, sandstone

Nile: faience, quartz, small and smooth river pebbles

Nephthys: faience, labradorite, hematite, color-shifting stones

Set: faience, red stones like carnelian, yellow stones, desert rocks and pebbles

Starry Sky of Nut: faience, lapis lazuli or sodalite

Khepera: faience, olivine, other green stones

Sistrum: faience or turquoise

Anupu: faience, obsidian, hematite

Horus: faience, lapis lazuli, gold, silver, bronze, turquoise

Wadjet: faience, bone or ivory

Barque of Ra: faience, resin, quartz crystal, amber, citrine

Feather of Maat: faience, bronze

Pyramids: faience, rock or stone, noncrystalline quartz

Union of Isis and Osiris: faience, two-colored stone, clay

Heqet: faience, green steatite, jade, olivine

Min: faience, gold

Ushabti: faience, steatite

Incense Bowl: faience, clay, resin

Sphinx: faience, rock or stone, noncrystalline quartz, sandstone

Selqet: faience, carnelian, gold, red jasper, blue glass, lapis lazuli

Appendix III
Quick Reference to
Scarab Symbols

 Ankh (p. 57)

 Anupu the Jackal (p. 75)

 Bast the Cat (p. 55)

Beetle *see* Khepera (p. 71)

Bowl *see* Incense Bowl (p. 97)

Cat *see* Bast (p. 55)

Crocodile *see* Sobek (p. 33)

 Crook and Flail of Osiris (p. 43)

 Feather of Maat (p. 83)

Hawk *see* Horus (p. 77)

 Heqet the Frog (p. 89)

 Horus the Falcon (p. 77)

Ibis Bird *see* Tahuti (p. 51)

Incense Bowl (p. 97)

Jackal *see* Anupu (p. 75)

 Khepera (p. 71)

 Lotus (p. 31)

 Min (p. 91)

Mummy *see* Ushabti (p. 93)

 Nephthys (p. 63)

 Nile (p. 61)

 Palm Tree (p. 37)

Pyramids (p. 85)

Scorpion *see* Serqet (p. 103)

 Serqet the Scorpion (p. 103)

 Seshat, Lady of Writing (p. 47)

 Set (p. 67)

 Shen (p. 49)

 Sistrum of Hathor (p. 73)

 Sobek the Crocodile (p. 33)

 Solar Barque of Ra (p. 81)

Sphinx (p. 99)

 Starry Sky of Nut (p. 69)

 Tahuti the Ibis (p. 51)

 Temple (p. 59)

 Throne of Isis (p. 39)

Throne, Crook and Flail *see* Union of Isis and Osiris (p. 87)

 Union of Isis and Osiris (p. 87)

 Ushabti (p. 93)

Wadjet the Cobra (p. 79)

BIBLIOGRAPHY

Ammer, Christine. *It's Raining Cats and Dogs and Other Beastly Expressions.* New York: The Intrepid Linguist Library, Laurel Books, Dell Publishing, 1989.

Andrews, Carol. *Amulets of Ancient Egypt.* Austin, Texas: University of Texas Press, 1994.

Ben-Tor, Daphna. *The Scarab: A Reflection of Ancient Egypt.* Jerusalem: The Israel Museum, Jerusalem, 1993.

Budge, E. A. Wallis. *The Mummy.* New York: Collier Books/ Macmillan Company, 1972.

Cambefort, Yves. "Beetles as a religious symbol." *Cultural Entomology Digest* No. 2:15–21, 1994. Available also online at the CED website at http://www.insects.org /ced2/beetles_rel_sym.html.

Evans, Elaine A. McClurg Museum: Ancient Egypt—The Sacred Scarab. University of Tennessee, Knoxville. Website: http://mcclurgmuseum.utk.edu/permex/egypt/egs-text.htm

Faulkner, R. O. *The Ancient Egyptian Book of the Dead*. Austin, Texas: University of Texas Press, 1990.

————. *The Ancient Egyptian Pyramid Texts Aris & Phillips Edition*. Oxford University Press, 1969.

Giveon, Raphael. *Scarabs from Recent Exhibitions in Israel*. Gottingen: Vandenhoeck u. Ruprecht, 1988.

Hart, George. *A Dictionary of Egyptian Gods and Goddesses*. London, Boston, and Henley: Routledge and Kegan Paul, 1986.

Petrie, Sir W. M. *Flinders Historical Scarabs: A Series of Drawings from the Principal Collections*. Chicago: Ares Publishers Inc., 1976 (reprint of the London 1889 edition).

————. *Flinders Scarabs and Cylinders with Names*. Warminster, England: Aris & Phillips Ltd., 1978 (reprint of 1917 edition).

Pinch, Geraldine. *Magic in Ancient Egypt*. Austin, Texas: University of Texas Press, 1994.

Sarr, John. *Introduction to Egyptian Hieroglyphics*. AIA Workshop Booklet, 1999.

Wakeling, T. G. *Forged Egyptian Antiquities*. London: Adam and Charles Black, 1912.

Zauzich, Karl-Theodor. *Hieroglyphs Without Mystery: An Introduction to Ancient Egyptian Writing*. Translated and adapted by Ann Macy Roth. Austin, Texas: University of Texas Press, 1992.

INDEX

☽ REACH FOR THE MOON

Llewellyn publishes hundreds of books on your favorite subjects! To get these exciting books, including the ones on the following pages, check your local bookstore or order them directly from Llewellyn.

Order by Phone
- Call toll-free within the U.S. and Canada, 1-800-THE MOON
- In Minnesota, call (651) 291-1970
- We accept VISA, MasterCard, and American Express

Order by Mail
- Send the full price of your order (MN residents add 7% sales tax) in U.S. funds, plus postage & handling to:
  Llewellyn Worldwide
  P.O. Box 64383, Dept. 0-7387-0108-4
  St. Paul, MN 55164–0383, U.S.A.

Postage & Handling
- **Standard** (U.S., Mexico, & Canada)
If your order is:
  $20.00 or under, add $5.00
  $20.01–$100.00, add $6.00
  Over $100, shipping is free
(Continental U.S. orders ship UPS. AK, HI, PR, & P.O. Boxes ship USPS 1st class. Mex. & Can. ship PMB.)
- **Second Day Air** (Continental U.S. only): $10.00 for one book + $1.00 per each additional book
- **Express** (AK, HI, & PR only) [Not available for P.O. Box delivery. For street address delivery only.]: $15.00 for one book + $1.00 per each additional book
- **International Surface Mail:** Add $1.00 per item
- **International Airmail:** Books—Add the retail price of each item; Non-book items—Add $5.00 per item

Please allow 4–6 weeks for delivery on all orders.
Postage and handling rates subject to change.

Discounts
We offer a 20% discount to group leaders or agents. You must order a minimum of 5 copies of the same book to get our special quantity price.

Free Catalog
Get a free copy of our color catalog, *New Worlds of Mind and Spirit.* Subscribe for just $10.00 in the United States and Canada ($30.00 overseas, airmail). Many bookstores carry *New Worlds*—ask for it!

Visit our website at www.llewellyn.com for more information.

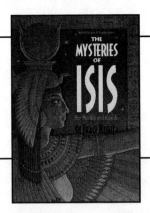

The Mysteries of Isis
Her Worship and Magick

deTraci Regula

For 6,000 years, Isis has been worshipped as a powerful yet benevolent goddess who loves and cares for those who call on Her. Here, for the first time, Her secrets and mysteries are revealed in an easy-to-understand form so you can bring the power of this great and glorious goddess into your life.

Mysteries of Isis is filled with practical information on the modern practice of Isis' worship. Other books about Isis treat her as an entirely Egyptian goddess, but this book reveals that she is a universal goddess with many faces, who has been present in all places and in all times.

Simple yet effective rituals and exercises will show you how to forge your unique personal alliance with Isis:

- prepare for initiation into her four key mysteries
- divine the future using the Sacred Scarabs
- perform purification and healing rites
- celebrate her holy days
- travel to your own inner temple
- cast love spells
- create your own tools and amulets, and much more!

Take Isis as your personal goddess and your worship and connection with the divine will be immeasurably enriched.

1-56178-560-6
320 pp., 7 x 10, illus. $19.95

Isis Magic

Cultivating a Relationship with the Goddess of 10,000 Names

M. Isidora Forrest

Divine Mother, Mistress of Magic, Goddess of the Green Earth, Queen of the Mysteries, Goddess of Women and Sacred Sexuality, Lady of Hermetic Wisdom . . . *Isis Magic* begins with a fascinating history of the worship of this many-aspected lady of 10,000 names. Apply this knowledge to a four-part initiatory journey through the "House of Isis." Through a series of exercises, meditations, and fully scripted rituals, you will come to know the heart of Isis. On a spiritual level, this process fosters personal growth and self-transformation. On a practical level, you will increase your magical and Priest/esscraft skills as you learn Isiac ways of healing, celebrating the seasons, honoring life passages, practicing divination, and more. Enter this four-part initiatory journey, and . . .

- Find out how Isis inspired England's Virgin Queen, Elizabeth I
- Discover what modern Priestesses and Priests say about their relationship with Isis
- Learn how to "Open the Ways" to Isis
- Powerfully connect with Her through special invocations and prayers
- Receive inner guidance by channeling the voice of the Goddess
- Ritually express and heal deep sorrows

1-56718-286-0
640 pp., 8 x 10, 13 illus. $29.95

To order, call 1-800-THE MOON
Prices subject to change without notice

The Sacred Tradition in Ancient Egypt

The Esoteric Wisdom Revealed

ROSEMARY CLARK

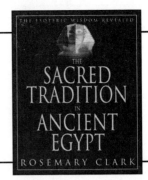

Our modern quest for the wisdom of ancient Egypt centers on the true meaning of the symbolism, temples, tombs, and pyramids of this enigmatic motherland.

Egyptologist Rosemary Clark, who reads Egyptian hieroglyphics firsthand, examines the esoteric tradition of Egypt in remarkable detail. She explores dimensions of the language, cosmology, and temple life to show that a sacred mandate—the transformation of the human condition into its original cosmic substance—formed the foundation of Egypt's endeavors and still has great relevance today.

In addition, *The Sacred Tradition in Ancient Egypt* outlines the technology that utilized cyclic resonance, ritual, and sacred architecture to effect this ultimate stage in human evolution.

1-56718-129-5

576 pp., 7½ x 9⅛, 68 illus. $24.95

The Tarots of the Sphynx

Silvana Alasia

The land of Egypt—its secrets, exotic and mysterious, shrouded in time, are hidden in the sands, guarded and symbolized by the enigmatic Sphynx. Ancient Egypt conjures images of a magical and distant world. Egyptian art is instantly recognizable and has inspired many occultists who in turn shaped the future of the Tarot. In fact, the modern Tarot owes much to Egyptian iconography. Hence, it is appropriate that artist Silvana Alasia consulted original Egyptian art to create this powerful deck. *The Tarots of the Sphynx* dresses the traditional Major and Minor Arcanas in new, yet actually old, images. All cards are titled in Italian, English, French, German, and Spanish. This deck will inspire and aid any diviner interested in exploring the past and foretelling the future.

Boxed deck includes 78 full-color cards and
14-pp. fold-out instruction sheet in English

ISBN 0-7387-0009-6
$19.95 U.S. • $29.95 Can.

To order, call 1-800-THE MOON
Prices subject to change without notice

Egyptian Tarots

SILVANA ALASIA

Amazingly detailed and gracefully beautiful, Alasia's tempera-on-papyrus paintings meld the stunning style of ancient Egyptian art with the mysteries of the Tarot. The cards come alive with stately, muted tones evocative of this ancient desert culture. To shape the interpretations, Alasia relied on the conceptions of Jean-Baptiste Pitois, who linked the Tarot tradition to the legendary Book of Thoth, a work fundamental to Egyptian magic. Replete with ancient and exotic symbols, these cards speak to the soul. The Major Arcana follow the traditional Tarot symbolism. The pips are rendered in the Marseilles style, with elegant Egyptian embellishments sprinkled throughout. This deck will easily transport you to a distant time and place where magic permeates the perfumed air. Once there, divination will be effortless and the unknown will reveal itself. Go there, if you dare.

Boxed deck includes 78 full-color cards and 9 cards and instructions
in English, Italian, French, German, and Spanish

ISBN 0-7387-0010-X
$19.95 U.S. • $29.95 Can.

To order, call 1-800-THE MOON
Prices subject to change without notice

Esoteric Ancient Tarots

ETTEILLA

A very unusual and historically significant deck, these cards were designed in 1870 by occultist Françoise Alliette, known in esoteric circles as Etteilla (Alliette spelled backwards). Etteilla, an established fortuneteller, was one of the first to popularize the use of Tarot for divination and the practice of interpreting reversed cards. The pips follow the Marseilles style and are ornamented with an arrangement of the respective suit symbols. The Major Arcana contains cards that use traditional imagery as well as cards that are completely original. All of the cards are renumbered using Etteilla's "rectified" system, so that even the traditional Major Arcana sport different numbers. Reflecting Etteilla's proclivity for Egyptian culture and the pre-Revolutionary period in France, the art is a striking blend of classical and Egyptian elements. Reflective of the divinatory style of the era, each card is labeled with a key word for both upright and reversed meanings.

Boxed deck includes 78 full-color cards and 9 cards with instructions
in English, Italian, French, German, and Spanish

ISBN 0-7387-0017-7
$19.95 U.S. • $29.95 Can.

To order, call 1-800-THE MOON
Prices subject to change without notice

Nefertari's Tarots

Silvana Alasia

Nefertari, the bride of Ramses II, assisted her husband in the temporal ruling of Egypt and lends her name to this most sumptuous and luxurious of all Tarot decks. During her incredible life, she witnessed the great expansion of her country and enjoyed the worship of her devoted husband. Upon her death, Ramses built Nefertari a stunning sepulcher that remains almost intact to the present day. This deck recreates the atmosphere and symbology so loved by Nefertari—she who is considered the Light of Egypt and a symbol of the most beautiful aspects of this elegant and sophisticated civilization. The typical two-dimensional Egyptian artwork is given incredible life and luminosity by the rich, patterned gold foil background. Each card is labeled in five languages (Italian, English, French, German, and Spanish). Drawing upon the fascination and mystery of Egyptian culture, Alasia has created a beautiful deck that is also practical for divinatory purposes.

Boxed deck includes 78 cards printed in gold
and 14-pp. fold-out instruction sheet in English

ISBN 0-7387-0020-7
$45.00 U.S. • $68.95 Can.

To order, call 1-800-THE MOON
Prices subject to change without notice